62 BRAND-NEW SCRIPTS!

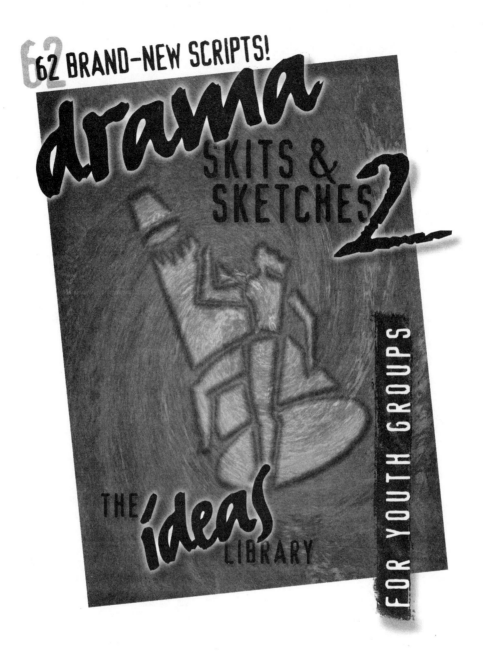

drama
SKITS & SKETCHES 2

FOR YOUTH GROUPS

THE ideas LIBRARY

THE IDEAS LIBRARY

Administration, Publicity, & Fundraising
Camps, Retreats, Missions, & Service Ideas
Creative Meetings, Bible Lessons, & Worship Ideas
Crowd Breakers & Mixers
Discussion & Lesson Starters
Discussion & Lesson Starters 2
Drama, Skits, & Sketches
Drama, Skits, & Sketches 2
Games
Games 2
Holiday Ideas
Special Events

62 BRAND-NEW SCRIPTS!

drama
SKITS & SKETCHES 2

FOR YOUTH GROUPS

THE *ideas* LIBRARY

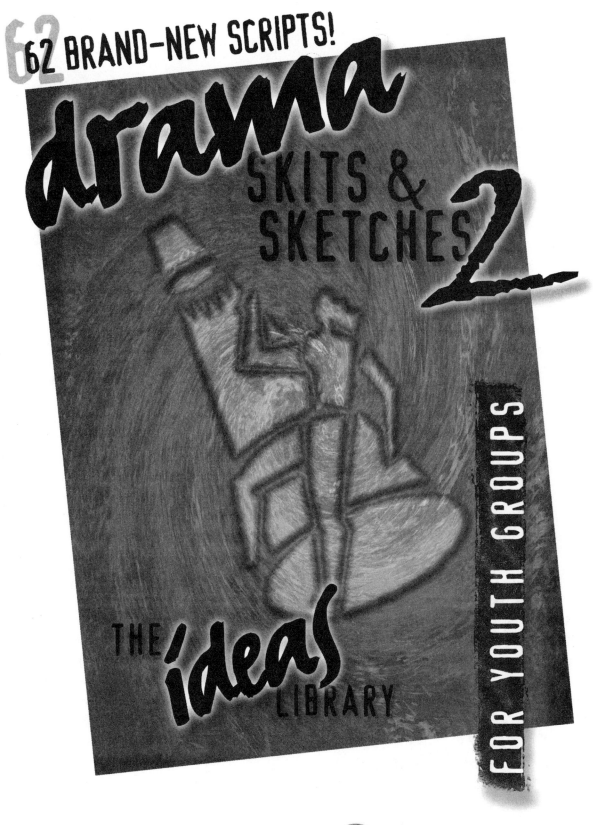

Youth Specialties

ZondervanPublishingHouse
Grand Rapids, Michigan
A Division of HarperCollinsPublishers

Youth Specialties Books, 300 S. Pierce St., El Cajon, CA 92020, are published by Zondervan Publishing House, 5300 Patterson Ave. SE, Grand Rapids, MI 49530.

ISBN 0-310-22027-0

Edited by Cheri McLaughlin
Cover design by Curt Sell and Mark Rayburn
Interior design by Curt Sell

Printed in the United States of America

99 00 01 02 03 04 05 06/ /10 9 8 7 6 5 4 3 2 1

CONTENTS

ALPHABETICAL LIST OF SCRIPTS

SCRIPTS BY BIBLE REFERENCE

Looking for a skit or drama for your meeting on faith? Materialism? Forgiveness? Dating and marriage? Salvation? Simply glance down the list of topics and find the perfect script for your purpose and for your group.

SKETCHES

Some students can tell Beelzebub from Barnabas. Others need help finding the New Testament. But the Bible is brought to life for *all* teens when they can act out scriptural episodes, stories, and passages. These scripts can be used as no-rehearsal reader's theater, memorized performances, or anything in between. (Other scripts that illustrate or portray particular Scriptures are indexed by Bible reference on page 6.)

THE PARABLE OF THE 10 BOY SCOUTS
MATTHEW 25:1-13

This modern setting for Jesus' parable exchanges 10 Boy Scouts looking forward to a camp out with the 10 virgins waiting for the bride groom. All that stands between the scouts and their camp out is a few C batteries. To be prepared to do this sketch on page 13, you just need flashlights and batteries. Or you can use it as a reader's theater or spontaneous melodrama by doing away with any props at all and having the actors read their lines. *Michael Noorman*

THE GOOD SAMARITAN
LUKE 10:30-37

Pull the Good Samaritan out of the hat once more. Only this time go with the twist that the script on page 16 offers. The man who was robbed and left for dead in Jesus' parable becomes a teenage boy whose best friend has given him the brush off.

Use questions like these to spur discussion after doing the skit:
• When someone was a good Samaritan to you, how did it make you feel?

• When was the last time you could have helped someone else but you were too busy or just not interested in that person? Would you do it differently now?
• Is there ever a time when we can do too much when we try to help someone?
Michael J. Hotchkiss

DO I HAVE WHAT IT TAKES?
A READER'S THEATER FROM EXODUS AND 1 CORINTHIANS

Feeling inadequate to do God's work is as old as Moses and Paul. Using the creative reading of two Scripture passages—Exodus 4:1-18 and 1 Corinthians 1:18-2:14—the reader's theater on page 19 meshes the struggle of those two heroes of the faith into a single reading. Recognizing that we're not the first to feel under-qualified and over-challenged encourages Christians to trust God's choice and to obey his call.

Place a reader on each side of the stage to underscore the dialog. The first reader uses the Exodus passage to question his ability to do what God has asked. The second reader responds with the 1 Corinthians passage, which sometimes offers answers and sometimes merely affirms the struggle. *Scott Davis*

HOUSE ON A ROCK

MATTHEW 7:24-27

Requiring very little rehearsal, this adaptation of Jesus' parable has more action than talk. With a saavy narrator, you could even use the script (page 22) as a spontaneous melodrama. *John Cosper, Jr.*

LIVING WATER

A DRAMA USING JOHN 4:1-26

Scripture comes to life in cast members the audience can connect with and a few contemporary touches. The script is on page 24. *Scott Davis*

THE COIN AND THE SHEEP WHO RAN AWAY

LUKE 15:4-10

Using an oddball combination of the parables of the lost coin and the lost sheep, show God's compassionate grace in action. The story plays best if the actors memorize the script (page 26).
Amy Norbie

THE MUSTARD SEED

MATTHEW 17:20

"God helps those as helps themselves" isn't in the Bible, of course. But sometimes mountain moving is less a matter of believing harder and more a matter of taking action, one step of faith at a time. This sketch (page 31) can be used to promote a mission or service project or to spark discussion of the kind of faith that moves mountains. *Teresa McCasland*

WHO AM I?

A good fit around graduation time, this sketch requires a bit of technological expertise to recreate the burning bush out of which God spoke to Moses (Exodus 3:1-15). One group videotaped the flame of a candle burning in the dark and used a large screen video projector to show the tape. Regular TV monitors are adequate, of course; it's just not as cool. After performing the script (page 32), play Margaret Becker's "Who Am I?" For an added touch, find the poem written by Deitrich Bonhoeffer from his prison cell in Germany during World War I. It's also called "Who Am I," and can be found in most versions of Bonhoeffer's book *The Cost of Discipleship*. *Scott Davis*

THE PARABLE OF THE 10 BOY SCOUTS

Matthew 25:1-13

• •

CHARACTERS
- Scoutmaster
- Narrator
- Ten Boy Scouts

PROPS
- Ten flashlights with batteries

• •

NARRATOR: And it came to pass in the days of Wal-Mart, Kmart, and other discount stores, that there were ten boy scouts…

SCOUTS: *(individually sounding off)* 1…2…3…4… *(etc.)*

NARRATOR: Well, there were eleven—ten boy scouts and their fearless, trusting leader, the scoutmaster.

As soon as they're done counting off, they start tussling and pushing and making exclamations.

SCOUTMASTER: All right, men…men! *(SCOUTS get quieter)* All right, men, I'm going to prepare a wonderful campsite for you guys. Wait for me to return—and remember our motto: BE PREPARED!!

NARRATOR: And all the scouts shouted…

SCOUTS: Be prepared!

NARRATOR: And the scoutmaster left, and there was a great sigh heard throughout the land.

SCOUTS: *(sigh)*

NARRATOR: Then night fell… *(offstage thud)* and the scouts began to organize themselves for the outing. They formed two groups: the wise scouts and the foolish scouts.

WISE SCOUTS: Be prepared!

FOOLISH SCOUTS: Chill out!

NARRATOR: Now the wise scouts…

WISE SCOUTS: Be prepared!

NARRATOR: …were sensible, thoughtful, and prudent lads. They had brought all the equipment they needed for a camp out, and most important of all, they all brought an extra supply of batteries.

WISE SCOUTS: *(turning on their flashlights and sweeping the audience)* Be prepared! *(flashlights off)*

NARRATOR: Now the foolish scouts…

FOOLISH SCOUTS: Chill out!

NARRATOR: …lived by a different code than the wise scouts. The foolish scouts were…foolish. They didn't think ahead to what they might need for a camp out. All they wanted to do was read comic books and eat junk food. They didn't prepare at all.

WISE SCOUTS: Be prepared!

FOOLISH SCOUTS: Chill out!

NARRATOR: And the really stupid thing was NONE of the foolish scouts remembered to bring extra batteries.

FOOLISH SCOUTS: Chill out!

NARRATOR: As night grew darker, the scouts turned on their flashlights *(flashlights on)* while they waited for the scoutmaster to come back.

WISE SCOUTS: Be prepared.

NARRATOR: And they waited and waited…and waited…and waited just a little bit longer.

WISE SCOUTS: Be prepared.

FOOLISH SCOUTS: Chill out.

NARRATOR: The scoutmaster still didn't come…and the night grew darker…and the scouts became tired.

SCOUTS: Yyaawwnn! *(one by one they wilt to the floor and fall asleep as the narrator reads)*

NARRATOR: One by one the scouts fell asleep, and none of them remembered to turn off their flashlights. Well after midnight, *(one by one the flashlights go off)* when the moon was high in the sky, someone shouted…

SCOUTMASTER: *(shouts offstage)* Hey men, I'll be there soon.

NARRATOR: The scouts woke up and found that their flashlights were out. How could they go on the outing with dead batteries? There was a flurry of activity as the wise scouts replaced the dead batteries. The foolish scouts, however, had no extra batteries. *(FOOLISH SCOUTS crawl from one person to another begging for batteries)* They begged the wise scouts to share batteries with them so they could be ready for the outing, too. But the wise scouts told them…

WISE SCOUTS: Chill out!

NARRATOR: If the wise scouts would have given the foolish scouts some of their replacement batteries, then no one would be ready. They would all miss the scoutmaster and not be able to go on the outing. Only the wise scouts were prepared. Only the wise scouts would be able to follow the scoutmaster on the outing.

WISE SCOUTS: *(turning on the flashlights and sweeping the audience)* Be prepared!

FOOLISH SCOUTS: *(irritated)* Chill out!

NARRATOR: The wise scouts told the foolish scouts that they could buy some extra batteries at the All Night Stop and Rob Thrift Mart. Just five blocks down, hang a left, go two more blocks…you get the picture. The foolish scouts went as fast as they could to the Thrift Mart. *(FOOLISH SCOUTS exit)* But while they were gone buying batteries, the scoutmaster returned.

SCOUTMASTER: *(enters)* Men?!

NARRATOR: The scouts stood to greet the scoutmaster.

SCOUTS: *(leaping enthusiastically to their feet)* Be prepared!

SCOUTMASTER: All right, men, let's go camping!

NARRATOR: And there was great excitement.

WISE SCOUTS: *(high fives, back slapping, and body slamming)* Yeah!

NARRATOR: And they happily left as the scoutmaster led them to the best outing ever. *(exit, still celebrating)* When the foolish scouts returned from the store, *(FOOLISH SCOUTS enter)* they found that they had missed the scoutmaster. They were really bummed.

FOOLISH SCOUTS: *(dejectedly)* Awwww!

NARRATOR: So what's the point of this little story? If you're not EVER READY, you'll be left in the dark.

FOOLISH SCOUTS: Be prepared!   **END**

The Good Samaritan

Luke 10:30-37

CHARACTERS
- Nathan, the victim
- Barbara, a passer-by
- Troy, a passer-by
- Sondra, the Good Samaritan

Scene: A busy street.
Time: One morning.

NATHAN: Two years with a friend and you think you know him. And then something like this happens. I feel so alone. My best friend has abandoned me. Here comes Barbara. I better not let her see me like this.

BARBARA: *(enters, recognizes NATHAN right away)* Hi, Nathan. I'm on my way to the kitchenware shop for a new cookbook. I just love cooking. But where was I? Oh yes. I saw you and said to myself, "Say 'Hi' to Nathan."

NATHAN: Hi, Barbara.

BARBARA: *(gets close enough to notice how he looks)* You look awful. You look bad. You look terrible. You look like I do when I've tried a new recipe and it fails.

NATHAN: It's a little more serious than that, Barbara.

BARBARA: I can't think of anything worse than a burned soufflé or a flopped main dish. I know I just want to die when that happens.

NATHAN: A friend left me.

BARBARA: Oh, that. I remember when a cooking instructor left our class right in the middle of the course. It was devastating. We not only didn't finish the class, we didn't even receive a refund. My world came to an end.

NATHAN: My friend's leaving was quite a blow.

BARBARA: You'll be silly if you give it another thought! Put it out of your mind! Go out and buy something for yourself. That's what I do. Besides, it was just one person—what did he matter? You're probably blowing it all out of proportion. I've got to go. I shouldn't have spent so much time with you on such a trivial matter...put a smile on that face. Bye. *(exits)*

NATHAN: Now I feel worse. Barbara thinks I'm upset over something trivial. What else can go wrong?

TROY: *(enters)* Nathan, have you seen Barbara? Somebody wanted to give her a message.

NATHAN: She just left. If you hurry you can catch up with her.

TROY: Thanks. So long.

NATHAN: Troy, do you have a minute? I've had something come up and I'm having a lot of trouble with it...have you ever been hurt by a friend?

TROY: One time and one time only and then I stopped it right there. I never made another friend. You've heard the phrase, "No man is an island"? Baloney! Every man should be an island. Simon and Garfunkel wrote a song called "I Am a Rock." That's my theme song. Don't let anybody get close to you. Don't even care about anyone. Don't make friends. It's the only way to survive.

NATHAN: Really?

TROY: I'm telling you, Nathan, if you ever let anyone get near to you you're asking for problems. Now harden up like a rock. Be like stone and stop this moaning and groaning. I have to catch Barbara before she gets too far. Shape up, do you hear me? *(exits)*

NATHAN: I can't believe it. Now two people agree that I'm overdoing it. Maybe I'm just exaggerating my loss.

SONDRA: *(enters)* Hi, Nathan. It's nice to see you.

NATHAN: Thank you.

SONDRA: Is everything going okay?

NATHAN: I won't go into it. Everything's fine.

SONDRA: If you want to talk about anything...I'm here.

NATHAN: So far everyone I've mentioned it to has been less than supportive. Besides, don't you have to be somewhere?

SONDRA: I can make time. Do you want to give me a chance?

NATHAN: Well, a guy who was like a big brother to me has started acting like he doesn't want to see me any more.

SONDRA: What's given you that idea?

NATHAN: He scratched my car two months ago and never arranged for it to be painted like he promised. He borrowed $30 over the past weeks and avoids the subject when I mention repaying it. He and I were supposed to watch movies together four different times recently and he's backed out.

SONDRA: Those are a lot of disappointments.

NATHAN: Yes, and now he avoids all my telephone calls and cuts short our conversations in person.

SONDRA: That can hurt.

NATHAN: I know this might sound trite to other people, but he was the kind of friend I could even discuss my girlfriends with. He took me seriously. He used to tell me about the things that were important to him, too.

SONDRA: I had a friend once who might as well have been a sister. When she moved out of state, I felt really hurt. I missed doing things together like we used to. I even felt betrayed, even though I know it wasn't her fault that she had to leave.

NATHAN: I feel a loss like that.

SONDRA: It's hard to live with the hurt and betrayal you're probably feeling right now. If you're like most people, you won't get over the hurt any time soon. You don't know why your friend has treated you like this. Maybe if you find out one day, it will make a difference, but today your feelings are hurt.

NATHAN: You're the first one who has heard me this morning.

END

Do I have what it takes?

A Reader's Theater from Exodus and 1 Corinthians

CAST
- Two readers

ONE: (Ex. 4:1) Moses answered, "What if they do not believe me or listen to me and say, 'The Lord did not appear to you'?"

TWO: (1 Cor. 1:18-19) For the message of the cross is foolishness to those who are perishing, but to us who are being saved it is the power of God. For it is written: "I will destroy the wisdom of the wise; the intelligence of the intelligent I will frustrate."

ONE: (Ex. 4:2-5) Then the Lord said to him, "What is that in your hand?"
"A staff," he replied.
The Lord said, "Throw it on the ground."
Moses threw it on the ground and it became a snake and he ran from it.
Then the Lord said to him, "Reach out your hand and take it by the tail."
So Moses reached out and took hold of the snake and it turned back into a staff in his hand.
"This," said the Lord, "is so that they may believe that the Lord, the God of their fathers—the God of Abraham, the God of Isaac, and the God of Jacob—has appeared to you."

TWO: (1 Cor. 1:20-21) Where is the wise man? Where is the scholar? Where is the philosopher of this age? Has not God made foolish the wisdom of the world? For since in the wisdom of God the world through its wisdom did not know him, God was pleased through the foolishness of what was preached to save those who believe.

ONE: (Ex. 4:6-9) Then the Lord said, "Put your hand inside your cloak."
So Moses put his hand into his cloak, and when he took it out, it was leprous, like snow.
"Now put it back into your cloak," he said. So Moses put his hand back into his cloak, and when he took it out, it was restored, like the rest of his flesh.
Then the Lord said, "If they do not believe you or pay attention to the first miraculous sign, they may believe the second. But if they do not believe these two signs or listen to you, take some water from the Nile and pour it on the dry ground. The water you take from the river will become blood on the ground."

TWO: (1 Cor. 1:22-25) Jews demand miraculous signs and Greeks look for wisdom, but we preach Christ crucified: a stumbling block to Jews and foolishness to Gentiles, but to those whom God has called, both Jews and Greeks, Christ the power of God and the wisdom of God. For the foolishness of God is wiser than man's wisdom, and the weakness of God is stronger than man's strength.

ONE: (Ex. 4:10) Moses said to the Lord, "O Lord, I have never been eloquent, neither in the past nor since you have spoken to your servant. I am slow of speech and tongue."

TWO: (1 Cor. 2:1-5) When I came to you, brothers, I did not come with eloquence or superior wisdom as I proclaimed to you the testimony about God. For I resolved to know nothing while I was with you except Jesus Christ and him crucified. I came to you in weakness and in fear, and with much trembling. My message and my preaching were not with wise and persuasive words, but with a demonstration of the Spirit's power, so that your faith might not rest on men's wisdom, but on God's power.

ONE: (Ex. 4:11-12) The Lord said to him, "Who gave man his mouth? Who makes him deaf or mute? Who gives him sight or makes him blind? Is it not I, the Lord? Now go; I will help you speak and will teach you what to say."

TWO: (1 Cor. 2:12-14, 7-9) We have not received the spirit of the world but the Spirit who is from God, that we may understand what God has freely given us. This is what we speak, not in words taught us by human wisdom but in words taught by the Spirit, expressing spiritual truths in spiritual words. The man without the Spirit does not accept the things that come from the Spirit of God, for they are foolishness to him, and he cannot understand them, because they are spiritually discerned. No, we speak of God's secret wisdom, a wisdom that has been hidden and that God destined for our glory before time began. None of the rulers of this age understood it, for if they had, they would not have crucified the Lord of glory. However, as it is written: "No eye has seen, no ear has heard, no mind has conceived what God has prepared for those who love him."

ONE: (Ex. 4:13) But Moses said, "O Lord, please send someone else to do it."

TWO: No!

ONE: (Ex. 4:14-17) Then the Lord's anger burned against Moses and he said, "What about your brother, Aaron the Levite? I know he can speak well. He is already on his way to meet you, and his heart will be glad when he sees you. You shall speak to him and put words in his mouth; I will help both of you speak and will teach you what to do. He will speak to the people for you, and it will be as if he were your mouth and as if you were God to him. But take this staff in your hand so you can perform miraculous signs with it."

TWO: (1 Cor. 1:26-30) Brothers, think of what you were when you were called. Not many of you were wise by human standards; not many were influential; not many were of noble birth. But God chose the foolish things of the world to shame the wise; God chose the weak things of the world to shame the strong. He chose the lowly things of this world and the despised things—and the things that are not—to nullify the things that are, so that no one may boast before him. It is because of him that you are in Christ Jesus, who has become for us wisdom from God—that is, our righteousness, holiness, and redemption.

END

H O U S E   O N   A
ROCK
Matthew 7:24-27

CAST	PROPS
• Narrator	• Graduation cap
• The Rock (male)	• Silly hat
• The Wise Carpenter (female)	
• The Sand (male)	
• The Foolish Carpenter (female)	
• The Storm (four females)	

NARRATOR stands off to the side. The other characters stand in a line and step forward as their parts come up.

NARRATOR: The Word of God is like a rock.

ROCK steps forward, flexes and growls.

NARRATOR: A rock that is strong...

STORM GIRL 1: *(feels ROCK's muscle)* Oooo!

NARRATOR: ... immovable...

STORM GIRL 2 tries to push ROCK over.

NARRATOR: ...and indestructible.

SAND hits ROCK in the stomach and winces in pain, holding his hand.

NARRATOR: Anyone who builds their life on the Word of God is like the wise carpenter....

WISE CARPENTER steps forward and puts on a graduation cap.

NARRATOR: ...who built his house on the rock.

ROCK gets down on all fours. WISE CARPENTER steps up on his back.

WISE CARPENTER: Ta-da!

OTHERS applaud.

NARRATOR: The rains came down...

STORM GIRLS stand around them and make rain sounds and motions.

NARRATOR: ...the winds blew...

STORM GIRLS wave their arms and make wind noises.

NARRATOR: ...and a tornado hit!

STORM GIRL 3: *(karate chop)* Hiiiiii-yaaaa!!!!

NARRATOR: But the house stood firm because it was built on the rock!

WISE CARPENTER flexes her muscles and growls.

NARRATOR: But the man who does not build his life on the rock is like the foolish carpenter...

FOOLISH CARPENTER: *(steps forward, puts on a silly hat, makes a dorky laugh)* That's me!

NARRATOR: ...who built her house on shifting sand.

STORM GIRL 4: That's you, partner!

STORM GIRL 4 grabs SAND, who is picking his nose, and throws him on the ground with an "Oof!" FOOLISH CARPEN-TER then cautiously steps up on SAND's back, struggling to keep her balance. Once she's up, the OTHERS applaud.

NARRATOR: The rains came down...

STORM GIRLS stand around them and make rain sounds and motions.

NARRATOR: ...the winds blew...

STORM GIRLS wave their arms and make wind noises.

NARRATOR: ...and before you could say "tornado"...

FOOLISH CARPENTER: *(falls down)* Aaaaaaaaaaaaaahhhh!!!!!

NARRATOR: ...the house came tumbling down.

FOOLISH CARPENTER: I've fallen, and I can't get up!

END

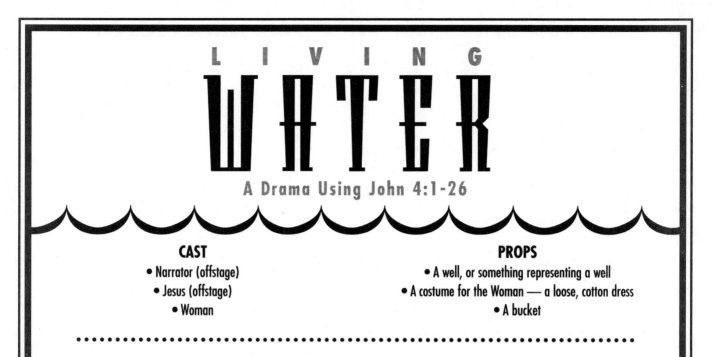

LIVING WATER

A Drama Using John 4:1-26

CAST	PROPS
• Narrator (offstage)	• A well, or something representing a well
• Jesus (offstage)	• A costume for the Woman — a loose, cotton dress
• Woman	• A bucket

Looking tired and sweaty, as if she's been working hard, the WOMAN stands beside the well, holding her bucket.

NARRATOR: The Pharisees heard that Jesus was winning and baptizing more disciples than John. (Actually, Jesus himself did not baptize anyone, only his disciples did.) So when Jesus heard what was being said, he left Judea and went back to Galilee. On his way he had to go through Samaria. In the Samaritan town of Sychar, which was not far from the field that Jacob had given to his son Joseph, Jesus, tired out by the trip, sat down by a well. It was about noon. All his disciples had gone into town to buy food when a Samaritan woman came to the well to draw some water. *(WOMAN enters)*

JESUS: Give me a drink of water.

WOMAN: *(looks up from the well)* How dare you ask me for a drink? I am a Samaritan and you are a Jew. Don't you recognize the situation here? We don't associate. Some people are just natural enemies—blacks and whites in the early South, Catholics and Protestants in Ireland, Jews and anybody…anywhere…especially Jews and Samaritans here today. Why, you people won't even touch the cup or bowl of a Samaritan. *(sarcastically)* We're unclean!

JESUS: If you only understood what God gives and who it is that is asking you for a drink, you would ask him, and he would give you life-giving water.

WOMAN: Excuse me, but you don't even have a bucket, and this well is deep. Where are you going to get this life-giving water? Purex? Our ancestors built this well, and it's been here a long time. Are you greater than they? *(sarcastically)* Are you some kind of miracle worker?

JESUS: Whoever drinks this water will get thirsty again, but whoever drinks the water that I give will never be thirsty again. The water that I can give you will become in you a spring that will provide you with life-giving water. It will give you eternal life.

WOMAN: You've got to be kidding me.

JESUS: No, not at all.

WOMAN: *(still skeptical)* Okay, give me some of that living water. Then I won't ever be thirsty anymore, and I won't have to come here every day and draw water.

JESUS: Go get your husband and then come back here.

WOMAN: I don't have a husband.

JESUS: You're right. You've been married to five different men, and the man you live with now is not really your husband. You have told me the truth.

WOMAN: How did you know that? How did you know that?! Who told you? *(regains composure)* I can see that you must be a prophet. Tell me this: My people worship God in one way, but you Jews worship God in another way and in another place. How should we worship God? What does he really want from us?

JESUS: Believe me, woman. The time is coming when people will not worship God the way you do or the way of the Jews. You don't even know who it is that you worship. You don't really understand the power and nature of God. At least the Jews know who they worship. In fact, salvation will come through the Jewish people. But you see, the time is coming and is already here when, by the power of God's Spirit, people will be reborn and worship God as he really is. They will offer him the true worship that he wants. God is not physical; he is spirit. And only through his Spirit can people worship him in a real way. Only then can those who seek him obey him with truthful worship.

WOMAN: I know that the Messiah will come, the Son of God, and when he comes he will tell us everything that we don't yet understand.

JESUS: I am he. I who am talking with you. I am the Christ *(the WOMAN gets a look of recognition on her face)*

NARRATOR: Then the woman left her water jar, went back to the town, and said to the people there...

WOMAN: *(goes out through the audience and speaks her lines to the crowd)* Come and see the man who told me everything I have ever done. Could he be the Messiah? Could he be the Christ? God's son? He told me things about my life that no one has ever known. You must come and see the man!

NARRATOR: So the town's people went out to see Jesus, and many in that town believed in him because the woman had said, "He told me everything I have ever done." They begged Jesus to stay a few more days, and many more believed because of his message. They told the woman, "We believe now, not because of what you said but because we ourselves have heard him and we know that he really is the Savior of the world."

END

The Coin
AND THE
Sheep Who Ran Away

Luke 15:4-10

CAST
- Chris
- Coin
- Farmer
- Woman
- Stacy
- Sheep

All characters line up on stage and stay on the stage throughout the sketch. CHRIS and COIN face downstage (facing the audience), ALL OTHERS stand behind Chris and Coin facing upstage (their backs to the audience). They stand from stage left to right in this order: WOMAN, FARMER, SHEEP, STACY. They "enter" (turn to face the audience and take a step forward) and "exit" (turn their backs to the audience and take a step back) from these positions.

CHRIS: Ladies and gentlemen. Imagine, if you will, that this is a coin. *(motions to COIN)* Coin number ten, to be exact, clutched in the grip of a careful and meticulous owner.

WOMAN enters. CHRIS stands between WOMAN and COIN, who have no interaction.

WOMAN: Six, seven, eight, nine... One of my coins is gone.

CHRIS: Are you sure?

WOMAN: Of course I'm sure. It's that silver one with the big nose.

COIN: *(feels his nose)* Big nose?

CHRIS: Coins don't have noses.

WOMAN: *(aside)* Can't you suspend your disbelief for five minutes?

CHRIS: Yes. I can suspend. Ladies and gentlemen. Imagine, if you will, that this is a coin—with a big nose.

COIN: Is it really that big?

WOMAN: It's just not here. My silver coin with the big nose—it's gone.

CHRIS: Carelessly dropped from the hand of his owner.

WOMAN: Excuse me, I don't drop coins. There's only one way for a coin to get out of this hand.

CHRIS: Do you mean... ?

WOMAN: I do.

CHRIS: Are you saying?

WOMAN: I am. He jumped.

CHRIS: So, the silver coin with the big nose has *FALLEN* out of your hand.

STACY enters.

WOMAN: *(to STACY)* Excuse me. Have you seen my coin?

COIN hides behind STACY.

STACY: What does it look like?

WOMAN: Oh, he's about so big, silver, big nose...

STACY: Hmmm...

WOMAN: He just jumped out of my hand. Why would he do that?

STACY: Maybe he wasn't happy. Maybe people told him stories.

WOMAN: What kind of stories?

STACY: Maybe they told him his owner might actually want to use him.

WOMAN: *(catching on)* And maybe they told him that being put to use would be painful.

STACY: But it's considered a privilege to suffer for one's master. And this coin must really be valuable if his master wants to use him.

COIN scurries from behind STACY to return to his original place.

WOMAN: Could it be that my coin is frightened?

WOMAN and STACY exit.

CHRIS: And so the woman continued searching for the coin that had jumped out of her hand.

COIN: Fallen. I had fallen from her hand.

CHRIS: After successfully rolling away, the coin found himself lying in a dirty street.

COIN: A dirty street! I wanted to go to the beach.

CHRIS: People were stepping on him and kicking him.

COIN: *(recoils as if being kicked)* Ouch! Hey, watch it!

CHRIS: A little boy with grimy hands picked him up...

COIN: Great.

CHRIS: ...and decided to buy a soda.

COIN: *(waving hands in front of his face)* Don't put me in the soda machine. Please don't put me in... ouch, ooh. Ow! Thanks a lot. That's why I jumped in the first place. So I wouldn't have to get used.

STACY enters.

STACY: Before long, someone else came to the machine and put in a dollar bill.

COIN: Oh, no. We're making change. Ouch! Ow! Hey!

CHRIS: Once again, grimy hands closed around the dirty, beaten up coin and shoved him into a deep, dark pocket.

COIN: *(eyes closed, hands feeling out in front)* Hey, it's dark in here! Hey!

STACY: But this pocket was different. This pocket had a hole in it.

COIN: *(drops into a low squat, holding his head)*

Whoa! Ow! Oh, my head.

CHRIS: And once again the coin found himself lying in a dirty street.

WOMAN enters.

STACY: His owner had been looking for him relentlessly ever since he jumped... fell out of her hand. *(WOMAN walks toward COIN as if searching the ground)* When she saw him lying in the street, dirty and beaten, *(WOMAN gasps in surprise, takes COIN by the arm to help him up)* she immediately helped him up and took him back to her house.

WOMAN and COIN exit together.

CHRIS: Not only did she clean the coin up and fix his wounds, but she called all her friends to celebrate because she had found her lost coin.

STACY: Meanwhile, back at the ranch, there was a farmer.

FARMER enters.

CHRIS: This farmer owned many, many sheep.

STACY: You'd think he could never keep track of them all. But this was no ordinary farmer. Still, there was one particular sheep who began to feel like a number.

SHEEP enters.

SHEEP: It doesn't matter if I'm here or not. Nobody would even miss me if I left.

FARMER: Is that what you think?

SHEEP: It's true! Sometimes I don't come when all the sheep get together to eat grass, and nobody ever knows the difference. One time I didn't come for three weeks, and no one even said they missed me.

FARMER: I'm sorry the other sheep acted that way. But you know I missed you.

SHEEP: Yeah, right.

FARMER: I did miss you. You didn't show up to eat grass with the other sheep last Tuesday, or the Monday before that. You've missed two private appointments to get sheared, and you haven't shown up for your personal daily grooming in five weeks.

SHEEP: Why don't you go show some other poor sheep the way? I'm gonna hang out around here for a while. Don't worry, I won't go far.

FARMER: That's what the last sheep who wandered said.

SHEEP: But look at all those luscious green hills over there. And down at the bottom is a foaming river. I hear it has a rapids.

FARMER: Who told you that?

SHEEP: Some of the other sheep. We never get to go to the rapids. We always drink from calm, still waters.

FARMER: You don't like the peace and tranquility?

SHEEP: Sure, I like peace and tranquility, but not all the time. Sometimes you gotta have a little excitement. I wanna see what the grass is like over there.

FARMER: I'm going back to the fold now. Are you going to follow me?

SHEEP: I'll be there in a minute.

FARMER exits.

STACY: So the curious sheep began to wander. Soon she had reached the far off hill where the "greener" grass lay, only to realize it wasn't any greener than the grass she'd had back home.

SHEEP: This grass looks a lot better than it tastes. Ooh, look. There's that river.

CHRIS: She ran down to the river. It was so beautiful! The water was swirling and foaming and splashing up against the rocks. Big, colorful fish swam by, and the sunlight glinted off the surface.

STACY: She bent down to take a drink, and...

CHRIS: Splash!

STACY: ...fell right in.

SHEEP: *(waves arms like she's trying to swim)* Help! I can't swim!

STACY: Looks like our sheep is in trouble.

CHRIS: It does look that way, but as we said before, this farmer was no ordinary farmer.

STACY: He had been looking for her all over the place, ever since she wandered off.

FARMER enters.

SHEEP: Help me!

FARMER: *(walks over to SHEEP)* Here I am. Are you okay? Come on. Let's go back to the fold.

FARMER and SHEEP exit together. As the next lines are said, each character turns just before his or her turn to speak and lines up facing the audience. SHEEP turns just before ALL speak.

CHRIS: The Bible says that heaven rejoices when a sinner repents.

STACY: Whether you've wandered from your Savior...

CHRIS: ...or have never even met him...

COIN: ...jumped from his hand...

WOMAN: ...or fallen.

FARMER: He's searching for...

ALL: ...you...

COIN: ...in the filthy streets...

SHEEP: ...in the deadly river that promised to be so much fun.

STACY: And he won't give up...

CHRIS: ...until he finds you.

FARMER: He loves you.

WOMAN: He will never force you to come.

STACY: But he will never give up...

WOMAN: ...searching...

CHRIS: ...for you.

STACY: The great Farmer...

FARMER: The great Shepherd...

WOMAN: ...wants to wrap his arms around you and tell you how much he loves you.

CHRIS: Like the prodigal son who began to apologize for running away.

COIN: "Father, I've sinned."

SHEEP: The Father prepares a feast and places royal clothing on your back.

STACY: And instead of asking where you've been...

WOMAN: ...he smiles and says...

FARMER: "My child who was lost has been found. Welcome Home."

END

THE
Mustard Seed

CAST
- Person one
- Person two
- Person three

ONE: Hey _____ , do you know what the Bible says about faith?
(insert name of TWO)

TWO: *(looks puzzled and shakes head "no.")*

ONE: It says, "I tell you the truth, if you have faith as small as a mustard seed, you can say to this mountain, 'move from here to there' and it will move. Nothing will be impossible for you" (Matthew 17:20). Do you think you have enough faith to move this mountain here? *(points to imaginary mountain)*

TWO nods head yes, flexes his/her muscles comically, then pushes on mountain as if to move it. TWO tries unsuccessfully three times, flexing muscles in between each try and looking more and more frustrated when the mountain will not move. THREE enters; watches TWO struggling to move the mountain.

TWO: *(noticing THREE watching)* Say…how much faith do you have?

THREE: I believe I have a lot of faith.

TWO: *(challenging)* Then let me see you move this mountain here!

THREE: Okay, you got a shovel?

END

 Copyright Youth Specialties, 300 S. Pierce St., El Cajon, CA 92021.

WHO AM I?

CAST
- Reader
- Juanita (a graduating senior, dressed in her cap and gown)
- God (offstage voice)

PROPS
- Bible
- A "burning bush" (perhaps a videotaped flame showing on a TV monitor)
- Graduation cap and gown
- Several differently colored masks that simply cover the eyes

The scene: Juanita, dressed in a (preferably) white graduation gown and cap, also wears a mask. On one side of the stage a video flame burns.

READER: *(reads Exodus 3:1-15. As the Scripture is read, JUANITA tries on a variety of masks.)* God is not forgotten in American culture—although it often seems like he's been forgotten. If he is not forgotten, though, he is regularly redefined and even officially "reimaged." The "I Am" of the Scripture is turned into the "What do you want me to be?" The result is that many have lost the sense of who we were meant to be. Who are you really? Do you know your identity? The "I Am" who called Moses is the same God who still calls those whom he chooses.

GOD: *(gently urgent)* Juanita, Juanita.

JUANITA: *(avoids looking at the flame)* Here I am.

GOD: Don't come any closer. Take off your shoes…you are on holy ground.

JUANITA: Holy ground?

GOD: Yes. Whenever you come into my presence, you are on holy ground. Now take off your shoes.

JUANITA: *(takes off shoes)* Who are you?

GOD: I am the God of Abraham, Isaac, and Jacob.

JUANITA: I've heard of them, but what does that have to do with me?

GOD: I'm also the God of…you—whether you realize it or not.

JUANITA: *(shields her face with her hands)* Oh.

GOD: What's that you're wearing?

JUANITA: Oh…it's my graduation gown…you see, this afternoon I'm…

GOD: No…on your face.

JUANITA: Uh…it's…a mask.

GOD: Take it off.

JUANITA: What!?

GOD: Take it off, too.

JUANITA: I can't…it's part of me. It's who I am…my identity.

GOD: *(unrelenting but compassionate)* Janita, take off the mask.

JUANITA: *(continues to shield her face and look away from the flame)* What do you want with me?

GOD: I want to talk with you about the plan I have for your future. I see you bringing my love and compassion to a sinful world.

JUANITA: Who am I to do something like that? I can't do it…

GOD: Yes, you can…and you will. I will be with you. I love you, Juanita. I not only made the universe, I made you. I know you better than you know yourself. I've seen the fear in your eyes and the insecurity in your heart. I know your lack of confidence, your weaknesses, and your mistakes. Juanita, I know your sin. None of that will hinder you when you're with me.

JUANITA: Yes but…

GOD: But what? Are you still clinging to your mask? It's not the real you, you know. It's merely the way you hide when the real you that I created gets lost. Juanita, you are my child, made in my image. Take off the mask.

JUANITA: But I don't want to lose my identity—you know, be a clone or a robot.

GOD: Yet that's what your mask does for you. Masks are Satan's sidewalk sale bargains—they're never one of a kind. Your mask conforms you to the world—clones you in the world's image of achievement and attractiveness. My purpose is to conform you to the image of my Son. Far from cloning, conformity to Jesus unleashes your unique potential. In contrast, that mask you're wearing now? It's dangerously limiting to your vision. Wearing that mask, you can't see what eternal differences you can make in the lives of those you touch. Nevertheless, I won't take your mask off. You must do it yourself.

JUANITA: How? It's such a part of me.

GOD: Peel it away…cut it off, if you have to! Authenticity is the first step out of conformity to the world. To share my love you don't need to be perfect, but you must be authentic. You will know security, not because you wear a steel mask, but because I Am the one who holds you in my hand. You'll know happiness, not because you wear a brightly tinseled mask of good fortune, but because I Am the source of joy. You are truly free only when you are free of masks.

JUANITA: Some people may not recognize me without my masks. What will I tell them about who sent me to them and about why I don't wear my masks any more?

GOD: Say to them, "I Am has sent me to share his love with you." When people ask you where your masks went, just tell them, "I Am nailed them to a cross."

JUANITA takes off mask.

END

SKETCHES

Off with the togas, on with the tank tops. Here are right-now, real-life scripts for everything from event announcements (that you can tailor to your own events) to dealing with emotional scars. Perfect for meetings, talks, Bible studies, even Sunday worship services. Use the "Scripts by Topic" index on page 7 to speed your search for the script that fits.

MR. SUBLIMINAL
PROMOTIONAL SKETCH

Very Important Note: Read all bracketed comments in introduction below quickly, in monotone voice, under your breath.

Why should TV advertising have all the great subliminal messages? It won't, once you use the script on page 41 to hype your next event. [Be sure to use it soon] In fact, I'll bet even now you can think of an event [next Sunday's dynamic lesson] to promote with your students using this sketch [call three kids to help], and all you'll need is a couple of rehearsals [call three kids to help]. *James West*

MR. SUBLIMINAL
EVANGELISTIC SKETCH

Body language, back masking, subliminal advertising. It seems we can never be certain that what we thought we heard was the message we were being exposed to. Could that work for evangelistic outreach as well? The spoof on page 44 helps us imagine what it might be like to lead someone to Christ using subliminal evangelism. The method may be humorous, but the message is the gospel. *James West*

READ THE BOOK

Use the whimsical script on page 45 to let your group know about an upcoming Bible study.
John Cosper, Jr.

WWJD?

Be certain your group understands that asking what Jesus would do could be tough on them—it was tough on Jesus. This drama (page 47) may even be in the making right now at one of your local schools.
Dave Tippett

Don't Treat Dad Like We Treat God!

Frenzied schedules regularly abort the time we intended to spend being with God, and more often our physical needs rather than our longing to know God drive us to his presence. The skit on page 50 places this dilemma in the context of a father/child relationship—a setting where our consistent disregard for God can be recognized as ludicrous.

Follow the presentation of the skit with discussion, using questions like the following:

1. What kind of relationship would you have with your father if you treated him like the characters in the skit treated their dad?
2. In what ways do Christians treat God similarly to the way the teens treated their dad in the skit?
3. What would happen if we treated our friends like the teens treated their dad?
4. What are some steps to building a strong friendship?

James West

Good Friday Service

Celebrating Good Friday can be for youths. What's good about a day when someone they're supposed to love was murdered? Not to mention that often they have an extra church service to attend during Holy Week. Try giving them a handle on what the Good in Good Friday means using the script is on page 53.

Karen F. Janzen

Signature of a Superstar
Ephesians 4:29 and 2 Corinthians 1:21-22

This easy-to-prepare sketch (page 56) gets your youths thinking about the value Jesus creates in their lives. The mark of the Holy Spirit—which is a human spirit being transformed into the likeness of the Son of Man—empowers us to live a life of love, a life of building others up according to their needs, that it may benefit those who listen" (Ephesians 4: 29). *Sam McKee and Steve Eisele*

Bucket of Light
Matthew 5:14-16

As the simple, no-prop skit on page 58 demonstrates, hiding your light in a bucket can be an attractive option among merciless schoolmates. What will happen to Cory, the new boy at school who's trying to light up the campus? You can either use the ending offered, or use the skit to kick off spontaneous role plays of campus evangelism—its hope and its horrors. *Dave Tippett*

Count the Cost
Mark 10:35-45

In this simple, three-person sketch, an offstage God talks with Marty about the cost of discipleship. The script is on page 65. *Scott Davis*

Grungeboy and "The Big Man"
Luke 9:26; Mark 8:38

Cut to the chase with this pointed story about judgment and about what exactly gets you into heaven (page 67). But be ready to respond to the inevitable challenge that a loving God wouldn't bar an "undercover Christian" from heaven. *John Cosper, Jr.*

His Strength, Our Journey
2 Corinthians 5:17

Like paper dolls, we can get torn and crumpled by those whose love and approval we need. The human way to survive is to turn the guilt we've been made to feel into blame of those who've hurt us. "If you hadn't…then I wouldn't." "I'm this way because my father, or my mother, or my boyfriend…" The drama on page 70 suggests another way to confront pain—a way that leads to wholeness instead of cycling back into pain. Since we've all been wounded, this healing process is, in fact, the human journey. It's our life's road we walk, but it's Jesus' strength that keeps us taking the next step. *Brett and Noelle Hadley*

Living with Unfulfilled Promises

Sandwich a hot talk on feeling let down by God between the two halves of this sketch. You'll find the story of Moses' disappointment in Deuteronomy 34:1-12, and Hebrews 11:32-12:2 surveys many people of faith who "died not having received the promises." The script is on page 73. *Scott Davis*

Many Parts

This is a great camp skit (page 76) with a point. Choose your band members and piano students to create this rhythmic lesson on the body of Christ. *John Cosper, Jr.*

Messages

The essence of the announcer's monolog on page 80 was taken from a Planned Parenthood public service announcement. In the spot a young man gives a clear message that sex is inevitable, and that teens have no choice but to give in and focus on birth control rather than choice. The teens in this sketch choose to make that announcer a liar. *Dave Tippett*

Never Alone

Although we may be blind and deaf to his presence, Jesus never leaves us alone. Only after persistent efforts to capture her attention does Jesus get the chance to encourage the teenage girl in the script on page 83. *John Cosper, Jr.*

Phone Chat

When it's time (again) for a discussion on the dangers of gossip, your group will get a laugh and a lesson from the script is on page 85. *John Cosper, Jr.*

Surf City

Want a comic illustration of the serious art of making a difference? Meet Kyle—channel surfing brother to P.J. You might be surprised at who takes the first step for better family relationships. This script (on page 89) readily makes sense to the unchurched, too. *Dave Tippett*

The Referee
Galatians 5

If you've got six people who enjoy playing pick-up basketball, you can use this sketch to tip off a discussion on living by the law versus living by the Spirit. When an overzealous referee invites himself to blow the whistle on overlooked fouls, the game becomes unpleasant. The script is on page 94. *Scott Davis*

The Test

The script on page 96 is a zinger—short, pointed, but not heavy. Viewers watch out! A teenage boy with the world by the tail is about to find out his girlfriend is pregnant. This short wake-up call should trigger animated discussion on sexuality. *John Cosper, Jr.*

Voices

"Voices" (page 98) could be part of an alternative Halloween event. The eerie presence of Death and the frightening anguish of Laura as Death amplifies all her failures as the ultimate trick, with no more treats—forever. Calling on Jesus' name breaks the hold of dark treachery on Laura and gives her the strength to resist committing suicide. *John Cosper, Jr.*

ON LINE

Who says God doesn't communicate audibly any more? In the script on page 101, Shelly hears God's voice in the a computer nerd's running commentary on her Internet woes. *John Cosper, Jr.*

THE VOICE OF GOD

Your church's Sunday morning worship service is the setting of this effective, though somewhat risky, drama. Every three to five minutes during the worship service, an offstage, miked voice representing the voice of God calls the name of the various people leading the morning worship.

While the associate pastor is making the announcements, for instance, the voice calls her or his name. The voice calls the name of a deacon who's taking the offering, a musician who's in the middle of accompanying a song, the pastor leading the morning prayer. These leaders, clued in ahead of time, act completely oblivious to the voice at all times.

Finally, as the Scripture is being read just before the sermon, the interaction scripted on page 104 occurs among the Scripture reader and four actors speaking from the congregation. *Scott Davis*

THE WAITER

Christ taught that serving others is the same as serving him. Jesus comes to visit a waiter at a busy restaurant in the skit on page 106. Jesus is a customer, and so are six other people primed for their parts and scattered throughout the audience. Passages like Ephesians 2:4-10, Matthew 23:11, or Matthew 25:34-40 provide a Scripture lesson to read aloud following the play. *Scott Davis*

Mister Subliminal

Promotional Sketch

CAST
- Mr. Subliminal
- Guy one
- Guy two

MR. SUBLIMINAL says everything in brackets quickly, in monotone voice under his breath, but loudly and clearly enough for the audience to hear.

MR. SUBLIMINAL: Hey guys, what's up? *(acts real happy)*

GUY 1: Nothin' much. What's up with you?

GUY 2: Yeah, you look like you're doing real good today.

GUY 1: Yeah, why are you so happy?

MR. SUBLIMINAL: Well, I met this awesome woman last Sunday morning.
[at _____] She's really nice.
      (name of class or group)

GUY 2: *(acts dumbfounded, as if he is wondering what inspired him to ask this question)*
Say, did you happen to meet her at _____ ?
                                       (same class or group)

MR. SUBLIMINAL: Yeah, how did you know about _____?
[lots of fun]   *(same class or group)*

GUY 2: Well, I don't know.

GUY 1: Say, I heard that it's lots of fun. *(dumbfounded)*

MR. SUBLIMINAL: Where did you hear that about _____ ?
[fun activities]   *(same class or group)*

GUY 1: I don't know, but I heard that they had a lot of fun activities.

GUY 2: That's funny, I seem to recall hearing that somewhere, too.

MR. SUBLIMINAL: Yeah, it's all right. [ask about this Saturday] We meet every Sunday morning. We have our own _____ . [ask about this
(activity, i.e., volleyball game)

_____] We also have our own drama team. [ask about this
(day of activity you're promoting, i.e., Saturday)

_____]
(day of activity)

GUY 2: Say, is _____ doing anything this _____?
(same class or group)   *(day of activity)*

MR. SUBLIMINAL: Well, it's funny you should ask that [come with me], because the
_____ this _____ [come with me] is having
(same class or group)   *(day of activity)*

_____
(name of activity)

GUY 1: Would you mind if we come with you?

GUY 2: Yeah, I'd like to come, too, but what are you going to be doing at
_____?
(name of activity)

MR. SUBLIMINAL: I'd be glad to give you a ride [don't be late]. We'll have
_____ , [don't be late] a pig roast, etc.
(list activity events)

GUY 1: What time can you pick us up?

MR. SUBLIMINAL: I'll [don't be late] pick you up at ___:___ [don't be late].
(time)

GUY 2: All right, we'll be ready and waiting.

GUY 1: Yeah, we won't be late.

MR. SUBLIMINAL turns to crowd and raises eyebrows as lights go down.

END

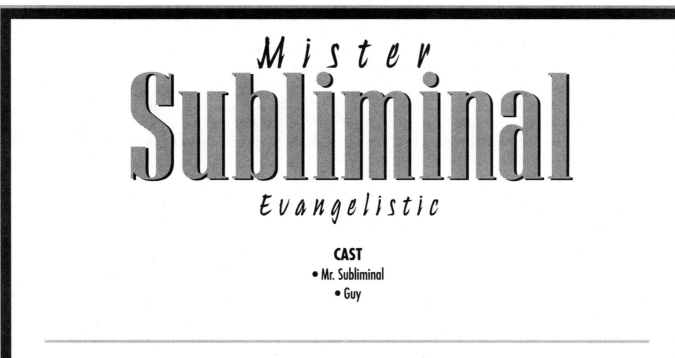

Mister Subliminal

Evangelistic

CAST
- Mr. Subliminal
- Guy

MR. SUBLIMINAL says everything in brackets quickly, in monotone voice under his breath, but loudly and clearly enough for the audience to hear.

MR. SUBLIMINAL: Hey, how are ya?

GUY: Oh, things couldn't be better. I'm doing just great!

MR. SUBLIMINAL: Well [no, you're not] that's good to hear [you're a mess].

GUY: *(suddenly starts to act depressed)* Well, actually, I'm not doing that great. For some reason it just seems like my life is in such a *(pause)* mess.

MR. SUBLIMINAL: Really, [something's missing] what do you mean? [something's missing]

GUY: Lately I just feel like *(pause)* something's missing in my life.

MR. SUBLIMINAL: I wonder [it's Jesus] if maybe you just [it's Jesus] need a good friend.

GUY: Well, yes and no. For some reason, I feel like I need Jesus. That's weird, I've never felt that way until now.

MR. SUBLIMINAL: So you think you need Jesus. [He's the answer] Do you think he can solve your problems? [He's the answer]

GUY: Yeah, I know that Jesus is the answer.

MR. SUBLIMINAL: Well, do you [admit you're a sinner] know how to accept Christ as your personal Savior? [admit you're a sinner]

GUY: Not really, but I feel so guilty for all the sin in my life, and I've tried everything to forget my problems and the guilt in my life. I've tried fast cars, a nice house on the lake, beautiful women, but when the fun was over I still didn't feel at peace.

MR. SUBLIMINAL: Wow, [he forgives] that does sound like a problem. [he forgives]

GUY: I bet if I ask Christ he'll forgive me, but I just can't bring myself to ask him.

MR. SUBLIMINAL: Well, [ask him] that's a decision you need to make on your own. [ask him]

GUY: You know, I think I'll ask him, but how do I know he'll forgive me?

MR. SUBLIMINAL: That's a tough question. [believe he died and rose again] I mean, [he died for your sins] I know some of the things you've done. [He came to save the sinner] If I were him, [believe he's God] I sure wouldn't forgive you. [He's God]

GUY: God is a God of love and he sent his son, Jesus Christ, to die on the cross for my sin and he rose again. Thank you, God. I just wonder if now I can have a relationship with Christ. I mean what do I have to do?

MR. SUBLIMINAL: Why are you asking me? [you did it] I mean, do I look like a theologian? [you're born again]

GUY: You know, I feel different already, as if I'm already a Christian, you know, born again! I admitted I was a sinner, I asked Christ to forgive me, and I feel he's done that, and I believe that he died on the cross for my sins and I know he is God and Lord of my life. I feel as if I've been…born again.

MR. SUBLIMINAL: That's great.

GUY: Well, I need to be going. I didn't mean to dump all my problems on you.

MR. SUBLIMINAL: That's okay. What are friends for? I'm only sorry I couldn't be of more assistance. *(looks at crowd and raises his eyebrows as lights fade)*

END

Read *the* Book

KATIE sits at a table drinking coffee and reading out of a Bible. GENA enters and sits down, drinking coffee. Dialogue is hammed up like a commercial.

GENA: Mmm. Katie, this coffee is wonderful.

KATIE: Isn't it, though?

GENA: What flavor is it?

KATIE: French Vienna Café Mocha.

GENA: Mmmm. Do you know what this reminds me of? Senior year.

KATIE: That trip to Paris!

GENA: That little sidewalk restaurant.

KATIE: With the cute waiter.

GENA: What was his name?

KATIE: *(cutesy)* Jean Luc!

GENA: What are you reading?

KATIE: The Bible.

GENA: *(surprised)* The Buh–?

KATIE: No, not the Buh. The Bible.

GENA: Why?

KATIE: Why? Because it's the most amazing book ever written.

GENA: That's a new one.

KATIE: But it's true! Where else can you find love, war, romance, comedy, poetry, prophecy, and history all in one volume?

GENA: An example...

KATIE: Take the story of the man who built a giant boat and filled it up with animals because God said it was going to rain.

GENA: What happened?

KATIE: Read the book. Then there was the prophet who was only allowed to eat food cooked over animal poop for an entire year.

GENA: What? Why?

KATIE: Read the book. And then there's the story of the Philistine town that was struck with a plague of hemorrhoids.

GENA: Hemorrhoids? In the Bible? How did that happen?

KATIE: Read—

GENA: —the book. I know.

KATIE: But most important story is about a Jewish carpenter, born in a manger, who died for you. And me.

GENA: *(cutesy)* Jean Luc?

KATIE: No, Jesus Christ. Anyway, there's a lot more, too. *(hands GENA the Bible)* Sixty-six books all about God and how much he loves us.

GENA: Incredible. Guess I ought to read mine more often. Hmm, where is mine? Last time I used it was in fifth grade.

KATIE: No problem. Let's go down to the Christian bookstore this afternoon. There's a new manager down there who goes to my church. He could probably give you a discount.

GENA: Not your latest heartthrob with the blue eyes?

KATIE: And that devastating smile!

GENA: What's his name again?

BOTH: *(cutesy)* Jean Luc!

Blackout.

END

WWJD?

CAST
• Three teen girls: Julie, Angie and Rachael

JULIE and ANGIE, dressed casually and carrying books, run toward each other from stage right and stage left and meet at center stage. Both are very excited.

JULIE: Angie! Angie! Did you hear?

ANGIE: Yes! That cute guy, that senior—Josh—was really a narc! And my cousin Andy and all his friends got busted in gym class this morning.

JULIE: I don't believe it! I talked to Josh…or whatever his name is…all the time! He was sooo cute. And nice. And funny. And—

ANGIE: It was just an act…to get close to us.

JULIE: But he looked just like any other kid.

ANGIE: Andy's really in trouble. My Aunt's really upset and—

RACHAEL enters and walks by, ignoring ANGIE and JULIE

ANGIE: Rachael. Rach! Wha—come here!

RACHAEL: *(reluctantly joins them)* Uh, hi.

JULIE: Did you hear what happened? That one senior, that Josh kid, was really a narc, and—

RACHAEL: Yeah, I heard. *(turns to leave)*

Look I gotta see Mrs. Kendal before next period—

JULIE: You got time. What's the big hurry? I talked to Josh…or whatever his name was…ALL the time. He was soo cute. And nice. And—

ANGIE: You said that already.

JULIE: Rach didn't hear it. Did you hear Angie's cousin, Andy, and his friends got busted and—

RACHAEL: Look, I really have to go. I'll E-mail you or something later, 'kay?

ANGIE: What's wrong, Rach? Something's wrong.

RACHAEL: No. Nothing. I—

JULIE: They say that Josh guy is gonna have some more names, and that Mr. Decker's going to tell all about it at a special assembly today.

RACHAEL: *(panicked)* Tell about what?

ANGIE: What's the matter?

RACHAEL: What's he going to say?

JULIE: I don't know. I heard he's gonna tell everyone how the cops got into the school and who's been arrested and stuff. Why?

RACHAEL: Oh no. They told me—

ANGIE: Rachael, WHAT is your problem? Do you know something about this?

RACHAEL: (quickly) No.

JULIE and ANGIE look at each other knowingly, then pull RACHAEL to side.

JULIE: All right, girlfriend, what's going on?

RACHAEL: I…I can't.

ANGIE: It's US. Hello? We won't tell. Come on.

RACHAEL: (tries to leave) I hafta—

JULIE: Are you part of this somehow?

ANGIE: Come on Rach, you can trust us.

JULIE: If you can't trust your friends, who can you trust? Now what's going on?

RACHAEL: (long pause, giving in) You guys have to PROMISE…and I mean PROMISE NOT to tell ANYONE, got it?

JULIE and ANGIE exchange glances.

JULIE: Yeah, sure.

ANGIE: Of course.

RACHAEL: (looking around) I may have to move away.

ANGIE: What?

JULIE: Why?

RACHAEL: (long pause) I'm the way…the cops…got into the school. I…steered them towards the guys who were dealin'. I—

ANGIE: You narced on your friends? Our friends? My cousin?!

JULIE: YOU turned them in?

RACHAEL: I HAD to!

JULIE: Had to? Rach, are you using?

RACHAEL: No! Nothing like that. I just told them who—

ANGIE: What?! Andy's my cousin! His life's ruined because of this! My aunt's going nuts!

RACHAEL: Listen! That Josh guy made friends with me. Said there was something that drew him to me. Something honest. Real. He saw my What Would Jesus Do bracelet and asked about it. I told him what it meant.

ANGIE: So you betrayed your friends…my cousin…to the narc because of your stupid bracelet?

RACHAEL: It's NOT stupid!

JULIE: Wow, Rachael. I…I don't know what to say.

RACHAEL: (looking at them) What did I do WRONG? He asked me if the bracelet meant anything to me, then he told me who he really was. And why he was there. To clean up our school. That there was a real drug problem here. And I could do something about it. Then he…he…wanted names.

RACHAEL: And so you gave Andy and the guys up just like that?

RACHAEL: NOT just like that!

ANGIE: He's going to JAIL thanks to you. How can you live with yourself?

RACHAEL: Andy's is going to jail because he sold drugs! I didn't send him to jail! He chose it!

JULIE: Rachael, when they gave us these bracelets in youth group, it was supposed to be for things like cheating on tests, and gossip, and arguing with your parents and...and...stuff. Not this.

RACHAEL: No. It's for everything.

ANGIE: *(grabs her own bracelet off and holds it up to RACHAEL's face)* It's for church, not for real life! *(throws bracelet to floor)*

RACHAEL: No. No! Don't you see?

ANGIE: *(starts to leave)* I gotta go. Gotta go find Andy. He needs me now. He needs REAL friends to be with him.

RACHAEL: *(after her)* You knew he was dealing, too, Angie. You never did anything about it.

ANGIE: *(spinning around)* Well, at least I didn't ruin his life over it. He would have stopped on his own. Don't EVEN think of us as friends again. Let's go, Julie.

JULIE: Rachael...I...uh...guess I gotta go, too. See you around. Or not.

They exit.

RACHAEL: Wait, you guys...wait. *(looks dejected, then slowly picks up the bracelet and looks at it for several beats...very quiet voice)* I forgive you. I love you. I did the right thing. Right, God? Right?

END

Don't treat DAD like we treat GOD

CAST
- Father
- Daughter
- Son

The whole sketch should have a time-pressure frenzy about it. Entrances and exits follow quickly on each other. Lights up in middle of conversation between DAUGHTER and DAD.

DAUGHTER: Dad, can I have $5 to go out with my friends tonight?

FATHER: That shouldn't be a problem.

DAUGHTER: Thanks, Dad, see you tonight.

DAUGHTER exits.

SON: *(enters)* Hey, Dad!

FATHER: Hey, Son, how was your day at school?

SON: Same ol', same ol'.

FATHER: By the way, I'm looking forward to going to the basketball game with you this Friday.

SON: Yeah, me too...Oh no...Dad, I completely forgot. I asked Kelly out this Friday. I'm sorry I forgot all about it. You're not upset, are you?

FATHER: No, I understand. How about this Monday's game?

SON: I'll have to take a rain check, Dad. I have a major exam Tuesday, and I need to study all Monday night. Dad, I'll make it up to you, I promise. *(SON exits)*

DAUGHTER: *(enters)* Dad, I just got myself into a big mess. I don't know how I'm going to get out of it. Dad, you gotta help me. I don't know what to do. I can't believe I was so stupid. How could I forget...

FATHER: *(grabs her by the arms)* Well, you haven't told me the problem yet.

DAUGHTER: Oh...well...I scheduled two dates for Saturday—how stupid! What was I thinking?

FATHER: Wait a minute. Why don't you go out with one in the afternoon and the other in the evening?

DAUGHTER: Dad, that's a great idea, but what about our date Saturday afternoon?

FATHER: Oh, that's right...well, that's okay. We can always reschedule.

DAUGHTER: *(hugs FATHER)* Thanks, Dad. You're a lifesaver.

FATHER: That's what dads are for.

DAUGHTER: You're the greatest! *(exits)*

SON: *(enters)* Hey, Dad, can I have $20 to take Kelly to see the Lame Brains in concert?

FATHER: The Lame Brains?

SON: Yeah, I see you've heard of them!

FATHER hands him the money and has a dumbfounded look on his face. SON exits.

DAUGHTER enters as FATHER remarks to himself...

FATHER: Lame Brains? Honey, have you ever heard of a group called the Lame Brains?

DAUGHTER: Yeah! That's a new Christian Speed Metal group. They're pretty good, that is, if you like speed metal. Dad, I need you to help me with this essay for English.

FATHER: I'd be glad to. What's the topic?

DAUGHTER: I really don't know much about the topic, but Mom says you are well-versed on the subject.

FATHER: *(acts a little proud)* Oh, yeah? What's the topic?

DAUGHTER: Mid-life crisis.

FATHER: *(acts put down a little)* Oh?

DAUGHTER: Dad...do you think you could help me?

FATHER: *(reluctant)* Sure.

DAUGHTER: Thanks, Dad. *(hands him the paperwork)* I need it by tomorrow night. *(starts to leave)*

FATHER: *(confounded)* Uh...wait...I...

DAUGHTER: *(leaving)* You're so awesome, Dad.

SON enters.

FATHER: Son, don't forget, I'll pick you up after school and we'll go out for an early dinner together.

SON: Dad, I can't. I meant to tell you we're having a student/faculty volleyball game today, and if we win the principal is going to kiss a pig.

FATHER: Well, son, trying to get together with you and your sister is impossible. Listen, when you and your sister have a spare moment, let me know and we'll get together, okay?

SON: *(leaving; in a jovial voice)* Kind of like, don't call me, I'll call you, right Dad? *(exits)*

Lights down except spotlight on the FATHER.

FATHER: *(discouraged voice)* Yeah.

Spot fades.

END

Good Friday Service

CAST
- Kelsey
- Greg

PROPS
- A church bench or chairs
- Two hymn books

Setting: on a bench in church. KELSEY enters, chewing gum obnoxiously, and sits down on the bench looking bored. GREG enters and sits down beside her.

KELSEY: 'Sup, Greg?

GREG: What can I say? I'm at church twice in one week. I thought Good Friday was a holiday.

KELSEY: From school.

GREG: At least when we have to be back here on Sunday morning we'll have lots of chocolate Easter eggs to sustain us.

KELSEY and GREG both take the hymn books on either side of them, open them up to the middle, and stand as if joining in congregational singing—but they continue their conversation.

KELSEY: I'm always looking for stuff I can bring to church to keep myself entertained. I tried doing my nails once—but the smell…

GREG: I usually count ceiling tiles or follow the blades on the ceiling fan. *(moves his head in circles as if following the motion of the fan)*

KELSEY: Boring is too colorful a word for it.

GREG: Do your parents make you come?

KELSEY: To church? Sort of…not really. I mean, we've always just come as a family.

GREG: Would you come if your parents didn't come?

KELSEY: *(thinks it over)* I guess so. I mean, I'm a Christian, so I come to church.

Copyright Youth Specialties, 300 S. Pierce St., El Cajon, CA 92021.

GREG: Why?

KELSEY: What do you mean, why? Why do you come?

GREG: I don't know. Family tradition, like you said.

KELSEY: At winter retreat Pastor Ken talked about coming to church to listen to God and be encouraged by other people.

GREG: Encouraged? *(snorts)* Who started church, anyway?

KELSEY: The disciples, I guess.

GREG: Didn't Jesus start the church?

KELSEY and GREG sit down and put the hymn books beside them.

KELSEY: No, I'm pretty sure it was the disciples.

GREG: But they started up the church because of Jesus.

KELSEY: Yeah, that's true.

GREG: And Jesus is the point of the whole Easter thing, too. Didn't he die today—you know, Good Friday?

KELSEY: That's what mom said. And he came back to life Easter Sunday.

GREG: Good Friday wouldn't have been good if Jesus didn't raise from the dead.

KELSEY: Why do they call Good Friday "good" anyway? It's depressing to me. I mean, you're right. This is the day Jesus was killed.

GREG: I don't know. It's really disgusting what they did to him—whips, nails, thorns. But he did it so we could be Christians—so we could get saved.

KELSEY: He went through all that for me. That really makes me depressed.

GREG: Maybe it should—at least on Good Friday. Then we have Easter Sunday. Happily ever after and all that.

KELSEY: So then are we supposed to feel happy or sad today?

GREG: Maybe a little of both. I mean, you don't want to take the crap he went through for granted.

KELSEY: True. *(she pauses for a moment)* You know, when I think about what all of this really means, it's pretty rude to call it boring. I mean, the tunes are way out of my style, and the preaching—but if you really think about the thing itself, the thing of Jesus dying for us, it means a lot.

GREG: So are you turning into a church freak now, Kelsey?

KELSEY: *(looks at him in disgust)* I think not! *(pause)* Maybe I'll just always let church time be when I think more about what's really going on with Jesus and God and me and stuff.

GREG: *(nods his head)* Maybe being in church all these years has already helped. I mean, we figured out what Good Friday was all about.

Lights dim to black.

END

Signature
of a
Superstar

Ephesians 4:29 and 2 Corinthians 1:21-22

CAST
- Michael Jordan
- Peter, a young boy having a garage sale
- Reader
- Matt (older boy)
- Tran (older boy)
- Tom (older boy)

PROPS
- A sign: "Garage Sale"
- A worn basketball
- A newer basketball
- Various other household leftovers

PETER sits beside "Garage Sale" sign with a few toys, a newer basketball and an old one, and some other junk. OLDER KIDS enter and begin pawing through the stuff with disdain.

MATT: This is nuthin' but junk! No one's gonna pay a nickel for any of it.

TRAN: *(points at the sign)* Uh… I think you're missing a letter on your sign.

PETER: What do you mean?

TRAN: You're missing a B. It should read "GAR-BAGE Sale." **(OLDER BOYS laugh)** We could sue you for false advertising.

TOM: How much for the basketballs?

PETER: Fifty cents for the old one, and five dollars for the newer one.

TOM: *(copping an attitude)* Dude, that old ball ain't worth a dime. It's balder than my dad. *(OLDER BOYS laugh)*

Suddenly PETER's face lights up and he stands, looking to the back of the church. MICHAEL JORDAN appears at the back of the church.

TRAN: *(following the gaze of PETER, looks to the back of the church, points and yells)* Whoa, that's Michael Jordan!

MICHAEL JORDAN: *(wearing sunglasses and taking long, loping strides, walks to the stage, smiles at the young boy, and gives him five)* How 'bout I sign that old ball?

PETER: *(immediately grabs the ball, hands it to JORDAN, and smiles hugely)* Sure!

JORDAN takes a pen from his shirt pocket, signs the ball, and walks off. Everyone stares after him open-mouthed.

MATT: How much did you say you were asking for those basketballs?

PETER: *(still grinning)* Five thousand dollars for the old ball. Five dollars for the new one.

CAST freezes.

READER: 2 Corinthians 1:21 and 22: "Now it is God who makes both us and you stand firm in Christ. He anointed us, set his seal of ownership on us, and put his Spirit in our hearts as a deposit, guaranteeing what is to come."

No matter how worthless or worn out we may be, Jesus would love to sign his name on our hearts. The world's greatest Superstar is ready to sign his name on your life, to autograph our hearts with his love.

END

B U C K E T   O F
LIGHT

Matthew 5:14-16

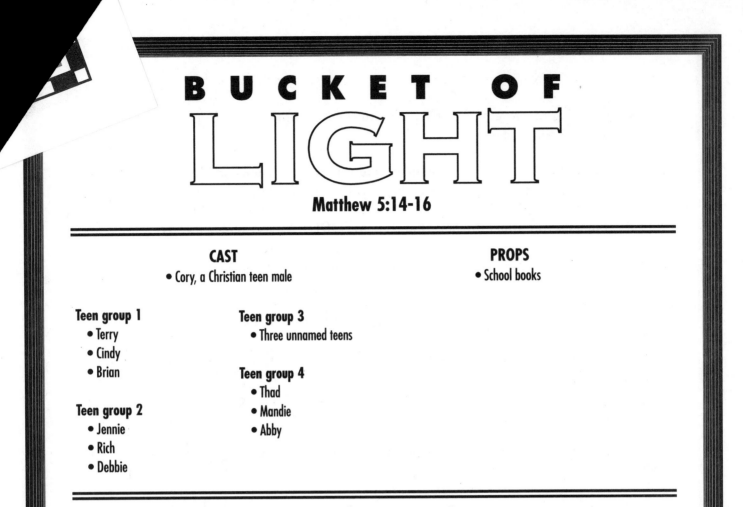

CAST
- Cory, a Christian teen male

Teen group 1
- Terry
- Cindy
- Brian

Teen group 2
- Jennie
- Rich
- Debbie

Teen group 3
- Three unnamed teens

Teen group 4
- Thad
- Mandie
- Abby

PROPS
- School books

Setting: *Four groups of teens mill around, carrying school books and aimlessly chatting. CORY enters stage left, also carrying books, and goes to the first group at downstage right. He walks from group to group around the stage. Watching this scenario in disbelief and shaking their heads, THAD, MANDIE, and ABBY cower into their own circle, obviously hoping to avoid Cory. He first approaches TERRY, CINDY, and BRIAN.*

CORY: *(with energy)* Hey, guys, how ya doin'?

TERRY: *(mocking his energetic delivery)* Oh, we're doin' just fine. *(the others in the group laugh)*

CORY: *(unaffected)* Cool. Hey, this awesome speaker's coming to our youth group Friday, and I wanted to invite…

CINDY: Yeah, right.

TERRY: No thanks, Jesus, maybe next time. *(the rest laugh)*

CORY: *(still "up")* Okay, no sweat. Maybe next time. Just wanted to make sure you knew…

BRIAN: Get lost, dork.

Copyright Youth Specialties, 300 S. Pierce St., El Cajon, CA 92021.

CORY: Okay. God bless anyway. Praying for you guys! *(wanders over to DEBBIE, RICH and JENNIE. They see him coming and ignore him)* Hey, you guys. How are you...

JENNIE: No.

CORY: Huh?

JENNIE: No. Whatever you're inviting us to, the answer is no. No, we don't want to go to your stupid revivals. No, we don't want to go to your stupid youth group. No, we don't want to go to your stupid church. When are you gonna get the message, Cory?

CORY: I just wanted you guys to hear this speaker. He's really great, and...

RICH: *(in CORY's face)* What part of NO don't you understand?

CORY: Sorry guys. Didn't mean to bug you. I just think this is someone you'd like to hear and...

JENNIE: *(putting her fingers in her ears and singing)* I can't hear you! *(DEBBIE does the same. RICH just glares at CORY)*

CORY: *(yelling over their singing)* God bless you guys! See you at lunch!

As he moves to the next group, RICH gives him the "loser" sign behind his back. GROUP 3, seeing him come, look up at each other and run off stage left. CORY shrugs and goes to group 4, which tries to ignore him.

CORY: Hey, guys.

THAD: *(looks away)* Whatever.

CORY: What's up?

MANDIE: Nothin'.

CORY: Hey, Abby.

ABBY: Cory.

CORY: I wanted to let you know about this awesome speaker...

THAD: *(hissing, looking around in fear)* Quieeettt, will ya?

CORY: Huh?

MANDIE: Keep it *DOWN*.

ABBY: Say nothing. Not here. Not ever.

CORY: What's wrong with you guys?

THAD: Just keep your voice down, will ya?

MANDIE: *(looks around)* Attract no attention to yourself.

ABBY: Be like the wind.

They all look at ABBY and she just shrugs.

CORY: What are you talking about?

THAD, MANDIE, and ABBY exchange looks, then pull CORY to downstage left, looking over their shoulders at the other teens.

THAD: *(looks around melodramatically; whispers)* This is better.

MANDIE: *(melodramatic)* Safer.

ABBY: *(ominously)* For now.

CORY: I don't understand.

THAD: Look, we've been at this school longer than you.

MANDIE: *(looks around)* There's danger.

ABBY: Everywhere.

THAD: At every turn.

MANDIE: Lurking.

ABBY: Ready to strike.

THAD: We could tell you some *REAL* horror stories.

MANDIE: Oh my, yes.

ABBY: The horror. The horror.

CORY: Stories? About what?

THAD: Who.

CORY: What?

THAD: Stories about who. Not what.

CORY: Huh? Who?

THAD: *(looks around, whispers)* Two words. Phil Richards.

CORY: *(loudly)* Phil Richards? *(the other groups hear him and look at him)*

MANDIE: Quiet!

ABBY: We're doomed!

THAD: *(nervous laughing, to other groups)* Not to worry. Just telling the dork *(indicating CORY)* what's what around here *(more nervous laughing)*. Ha ha ha. Ha ha. Ha. *(eventually, groups start talking among themselves again)*

CORY: I really don't like to be called names.

THAD: Sorry. I, uh, panicked.

CORY: So, who's this Phil Richards?

THAD: *(solemnly)* Phil.

MANDIE: Poor Phil.

ABBY: The Philster.

CORY: Is somebody going to tell me what…

THAD: *(interrupts)* Phil didn't make it. He was just like you. Outspoken. Open. Then one day…one day…oh, I can't go on.

MANDIE: *(hand on THAD's shoulder)* You've got tell him.

ABBY: Press on.

THAD: One day we found…Phil. Or what was left of him.

CORY: He…died?!

THAD: No. But he might as well have.

MANDIE: The…locker.

ABBY: A-12.

THAD: We found him there. Stuffed inside. Shaving cream on his head. Monster wedgie. His Bible in ruins. He was a mess.

MANDIE: A mess.

ABBY: I want my Mommy.

CORY: *(excited)* His Bible? Was he a Christian?!

THAD, MANDIE, and ABBY: *(looking around in fear)* SHHHHHHHH! *(the other groups look over again, and the three smile and wave weakly, making hand gestures towards CORY like he's crazy)*

THAD: *(quietly, hissing)* Yeesss. Phil dropped out of school the next day. His parents pulled him out. We never saw him again.

MANDIE: A trail of shaving cream was all that remained.

ABBY: Until Janitor Bob cleaned it up several months later.

THAD: The poor sap. *(pause)* Not Janitor Bob, Phil.

CORY: So, let me get this straight. Phil was a Christian, and he was persecuted for his faith? *(THAD, MANDIE, and ABBY all nod solemnly)* Well, praise God!

THAD, MANDIE, and ABBY: *(looking around in fear)* SHHHHHHHH!

CORY: But that means he was being effective! We should all be strong witnesses.

THAD: *(puts his hands over his ears)* No! No! No!

MANDIE: *(puts her hands over her eyes)* Stop! Stop! Stop!

ABBY: *(puts her hand over her mouth, mumbles)* Mommy! Mommy! Mommy!

CORY: *(studies the three standing there with their hands over their ears, eyes, and mouths)* So, should I assume you three are Christians, too? *(they all stare at him, with their respective hands still in place, and nod slowly)* What's the big deal? So we go through some persecution. God promised he'd get us through that junk. We just have to be faithful in telling others about Jesus, and God promises to help. Right? Am I right?

THAD: *(hands still in place)* Yeah, guess so.

MANDIE: *(hands still in place)* Uh huh.

ABBY: *(same)* Mffph.

CORY: Look. *(gently takes down their hands)* This school needs to hear about Jesus. No matter what. They're all dying to hear about him—literally. Come on, join me.

THAD: You don't understand…

MANDIE: It's just not me…

ABBY: I'm…sorry.

CORY: We need to be the light of the world. We're stronger together. Two are better than one. Three together are great. Four together…

THAD: My locker's too small to get stuffed into. And I'm allergic.

MANDIE: Ditto.

ABBY: I'm…sorry.

CORY: But…

THAD: *(whispers to CORY, arm around him)* Look, we've seen this before. A new kid like yourself comes in, starts being… *(makes quote signs)* "open"…about their faith. Then WHAMO! It's a date with Mr. Locker and Janitor Bob.

CORY: But don't you see…

THAD: Is there someone we can call, you know, in case you…well…

MANDIE: End up like Phil?

CORY: *(shrugs)* Well, if I end up like that, it's better than hiding my light under a bucket. Right?

They all shake their heads.

THAD: The bucket speech.

MANDIE: Been there. Heard that.

THAD: They never learn. We'll be *(looks around for an extended time, whispers)* praying for you. Come on guys, let's make a break for it. *(MANDIE stands ready, waiting. THAD looks around, checking for ambushes, then pushes her)* Go! Go! Go! *(MANDIE sprints off)* Come on, Abby. *(ABBY looks at CORY for a beat, then readies herself)* Ready…wait! Wait! *(TERRY walks by and THAD and ABBY wave. Once he's gone, THAD pushes ABBY)* Go! Go! Go! *(ABBY runs off. THAD looks around for an extended time, then runs)* Gone! Gone! Gone!

CORY watches them leave. After a beat, TERRY and BRIAN walk by CORY and push him out of the way as they exit. CORY falls back, then stands there, head down, looking defeated. After a beat, ABBY re-enters, and slowly goes to him.

ABBY: *(quietly)* Two…are better than one. Right?

CORY: *(looks up in surprise)* Huh? Oh, yeah. Right. Right! Thanks, Abby. Come on. *(looks offstage, and starts running that way)* Hey, you guys! Wanna hear about this awesome speaker we've got coming? *(exits)*

ABBY: *(looks after him, starts to turn away, then stops and runs after CORY, looking up)* Daddy! Daddy! Daddy!

END

Mark 10:35-45

CAST

- Marty, a successful, sincere God-seeker
- Angel, receptionist at God's office
- God

PROPS

- Receptionist desk
- Hat

MAN: *(walks in tentatively with his hat in his hands)* Hi. Ummm. I would like to see the person in charge, please.

ANGEL: Sure, come on in.

MAN: Look, uh, I know this guy is really important, and I know I don't have an appointment. Do you think he'll still see me?

ANGEL: He sees everyone. In fact, you can talk to him any time you'd like.

MAN: Do you think I could see him now?

ANGEL: Go right on in.

MAN: *(still tentatively)* Now?

ANGEL: Yes. *(motions him in)*

MAN: *(hesitates, then slowly walks in. As he talks with God, it's most effective if he looks over the audience toward the back of the room)* Uh... excuse me. My name is...

GOD: I know your name.

MAN: Uh...yes. I guess you do. Well, umm...I wondered if I could see you for a few minutes?

GOD: I've got all the time you need.

MAN: I know that when most people come to see you it's because they have problems they want fixed or because they're in some kind of trouble.

GOD: It's true. Many people come to me when they are hurting.

MAN: Yeah...well, to tell you the truth, things are going pretty well for me right now...I mean I have a good steady job, I'm making good money, and I've just met a terrific girl. You should see her, whoa!

GOD: I have seen her. I made her.

MAN: Yeah, of course. I forgot. Anyway, in spite of all the good things in my life, I'm still a little confused. I mean some of my friends talk about you as if they really know you, and I'm just wondering if maybe I'm missing something. Is there really more to life than what I know right now? I mean, quite frankly, I just don't see the point. *(begins to get a little bolder)* So, anyway, that's why I'm here. I started thinking, maybe you really are important and that I might want to pursue a position in your organization...maybe as your right-hand man.

GOD: My price is high.

MAN: Well, like I said, I've been fairly successful so far. Would you like me to write a check, or perhaps a money order for...what...two, three hundred?

GOD: No, that's not what I'm asking for.

MAN: Of course, that is a little low. Well, I have some liquid assets, and I could probably come up with a couple thousand without much trouble.

GOD: I don't think you understand what I require.

MAN: Look, we're both reasonable people here. Why don't you just give me the bottom line?

GOD: *(slight pause)* All.

MAN: *(shocked)* Excuse me?

GOD: All.

MAN: Did you say all?

GOD: Yes, all. Everything. Body, mind, and soul.

MAN: Sheesh! Isn't that pretty extreme? I mean what about a layaway plan or maybe an easy pay-as-you-go installment plan? Isn't your profit margin a little out of line?

GOD: Actually, my cost was quite high as well...Just ask my son.

MAN: *(mildly indignant)* Yeah, well, if you don't mind my saying so, it sounds a little greedy to me. *(calming down)* Look, I'll have to give it some thought. I appreciate your time, and I'm sure you mean well, but it's a little soon to be giving up everything for something I can't even see. Besides, I have a feeling I can find what I'm looking for at a little cheaper price.

GOD: Be careful. The price may be cheaper, but your cost may be much higher than you think.

MAN: Yeah, well, I'll think about it. Maybe I'll see you around *(begins to leave)*

GOD: I'm sure you will. I'm sure you will.

END

Grunge Boy
AND THE
BiG MAN

LUKE 9:26; MARK 8:38

CAST
- Announcer (offstage voice)
- Ah-mee (narrator)
- Grungeboy, Seattle grunge rocker
- Grunge record producer
- Grunge Girl, grunge music fan
- God the Father (offstage voice)]
- Jesus

PROPS
- Grunge CD — Pearl Jam, Nirvana or Poor Old Lu will work
- Clipboard and papers
- Sheet music
- Autograph book and pen

● ●

ANNOUNCER: And now, it's time for a grunge fairy tale, with your host, Ah-mee.

AH-MEE, dressed in a flannel and jeans, wearing a nose ring, etc., enters. Music fades out.

AH-MEE: *(rambling, spaced out)* Okay, so, like, once upon a time, right? There was this guy, and his name was Grungeboy.

GRUNGEBOY enters.

AH-MEE: They called him Grungeboy because, like, that's what he did, you know? He was into the grunge thing. He didn't start out like that, though. He and his friends started playing at their church, and they even named their band the Golden Hemorrhoids, after a Bible story. You can look up for yourself in 1 Samuel 5 and 6, 'kay? So anyway, they, like, got really good, and somebody told Grungeboy to try to get a record deal, right? So he did.

GRUNGE PRODUCER enters.

GRUNGEBOY: *(hands PRODUCER sheet music)* Hey, man, you wanna, like produce my record?

AH-MEE: Well, the producer, right? He really liked his stuff and all, 'cause like the Golden Hemorrhoids were really rockin'. But he had a question.

PRODUCER: What's the song about?

GRUNGEBOY: Well, you know, it's like, uh, it's about…HIM.

PRODUCER: Who?

GRUNGEBOY: You know. *(points up)* HIM. The big guy? The man upstairs?

PRODUCER: *(still not sure)* Okay, whatever. *(hands GRUNGEBOY a contract)* Sign here.

GRUNGEBOY signs. PRODUCER exits.

AH-MEE: So, like, the deal is, Grungeboy kinda wrote songs about God, only they didn't really mention his name or nothin'. And he never used the "J-word." 'Cause, like, Grungeboy was an artist first and then a Christian, and he wanted people to like him for his music. So anyway, like, the Golden Hemorrhoids went on tour with Pearl Jam, and Grungeboy had chicks all over him, which he thought was pretty cool.

GRUNGE GIRL runs on, holds out autograph pad to GRUNGEBOY. He takes it and signs it.

AH-MEE: So he, like had this great chance to share his faith, right? 'Cause people, like, dug his stuff and wanted to know where he got his inspiration. But whenever people asked him…

GRUNGE GIRL: Grungeboy, where do you get your inspiration? Is it some higher power?

AH-MEE: All he would say was…

GRUNGEBOY: Well, yeah, it, like, comes from…HIM.

GRUNGE GIRL: Who?

GRUNGEBOY: You know. HIM.

GRUNGE GIRL: Him who?

GRUNGEBOY: The Big Man? The Man Upstairs?

GRUNGE GIRL: Some guy in your attic?

GRUNGEBOY: No, no. It's, you know, J-C.

GRUNGE GIRL: *(gets it)* Oh, I get ya. *(GRUNGE GIRL walks to AH-MEE)* I didn't know Jim Carrey wrote music! *(exits)*

AH-MEE: So, like, Grungeboy wrote all this great music, but nobody got the point because he was like, too much of a wuss to tell 'em. Anyway, like all great rockers, Grungeboy died young, showed up in heaven, and saw—

GRUNGEBOY: *(looks up)* Hey, it's the Big Man! I was just workin' on a song for you.

GOD: Who are you?

GRUNGEBOY: You know me. I'm Grungeboy. I used to write songs about you.

GOD: Funny. I don't remember that. But maybe my son will.

JESUS enters carrying a clipboard with papers.

GRUNGEBOY: Whoa. It's…it's you!

JESUS: Yeah, it's me. And you are?

GRUNGEBOY: Oh, don't tell me you don't remember.

GOD: Son, do you know this man?

JESUS: Let me see. It was…no. Could he be…nope, that's not him either. Maybe he was…no, he's still down there working.

GRUNGEBOY: Come on, man, you gotta help me out!

JESUS: Sorry, man, I'm doing the best I can. Let me look you up.

GRUNGEBOY: *(to God)* Come on. Don't you remember me? I'm Grungeboy!

JESUS: I don't have any Grungeboy in here.

GRUNGEBOY: Well…what does that mean?

GOD: It means my son never knew you.

GRUNGEBOY: Come on, man! I wrote songs about you. I sang in front of over a million people! They all heard about you! I mean, I never mentioned you directly, but everybody got the message…at least, I thought they did.

JESUS: I'm sorry. I never knew you.

GRUNGEBOY and JESUS exit.

AH-MEE: So, like, the moral of the story is Luke 9:26, which says, "If anyone is ashamed of me and my words, the Son of Man will be ashamed of him when he comes in his glory and in the glory of the Father and of the holy angels." Or you could say it—if you diss Jesus to your friends, he's gonna diss you to his Father in heaven. The end.

END

His Strength
Our Journey

2 Corinthians 5:17

CAST
- Girl
- Mother
- Father
- Teacher
- Boy
- Jesus

PROPS
- Scissors
- Two identical paper dolls
- Four posterboard signs on strings with "guilt" or "shame" written on one side, and "blame" written on the other
- Red sash for Jesus

Set: The cast are frozen on an empty stage in the following positions: GIRL sits on the floor downstage center with, crayons, scissors and a paper doll. MOTHER stands downstage left with her hands on her hips; FATHER stands reading a newspaper downstage right, facing GIRL; a TEACHER stands upstage right, holding her Bible with one hand and extending her other hand in a comforting gesture; BOY stands upstage left, holding his jacket over his shoulder and grasping with his other hand the sunglasses he's wearing. JESUS stands upstage center, his arms raised and gazing toward heaven as if in prayer. Stage is in blackout.

A white spot comes up on GIRL. "Sesame Street" or other recognizably children's music plays. She finishes cutting out a paper doll. Pleased with herself, she begins to play with the doll.

MOTHER: *(comes alive and walks crisply to GIRL's spotlight)* Where have you been? I've been looking all over for you. *(GIRL holds up paper doll. MOTHER takes it from her and inspects it)* Awww, isn't that cute? Look what you've made, a sweet little doll. You know, your big sister made the best paper dolls. *(GIRL looks hurt)* I remember her cutting right on the lines and drawing the funniest faces on them. *(GIRL looks more and more dejected)* She was so talented. *(falsely bright)* Try a little harder, dear, maybe you could grow up to be more like her. *(MOTHER tears off an arm, returns the mutilated paper doll, and deftly drops a "shame" sign over GIRL's head)* By the way, don't let your father catch you leaving paper scraps on the floor—you know how his temper is. *(turning on her heel, MOTHER taps back to her original pose)*

FATHER: *(rattling the newspaper and entering GIRL's spotlight)* What are you doing here?! *(GIRL is obviously afraid)* How many times have I told you not to play in your good clothes?! Look at yourself! You've got marks all over your shirt. You're a sloppy, careless little girl! What's it going to take to get you to obey me, huh!? Only bad little girls disobey their fathers—and I won't have any of that nonsense in my house. *(snatching the paper doll from her, he tears off the head and slaps it back into her lap as he puts a "guilt" sign on her)* That'll teach you a lesson you'll never forget! *(GIRL crumbles to the floor as FATHER stomps back to his position and freezes)*

TEACHER: *(enters)* Little girl, why are you crying? Don't you know that God loves you? What ever your problems are, they aren't too much for God. *(mild, well-intentioned scolding)* If you would just pray more and read your Bible every day, all things come to those who believe. Maybe you just don't have enough faith! *(GIRL sits up and hesitantly hands over her paper doll. TEACHER takes it and tears off a leg)* You have to try harder! *(hands back the doll and hangs a "guilt" sign on her)* God only helps those who help themselves! *(returns to position and freezes)*

BOY comes alive.

BOY: Helloooo Chica. *(GIRL cowers and is obviously scared)* Hey, what's the matter? It's me — *(with a sinisterly sensual laugh)* your "father figure" from down the street. Did I ever tell you you were hot? *(she looks away; BOY sounds hostile)* Don't act like you didn't want it. Any girl wearing what you wore and putting on the timid female act is asking for it. Yeah, you wanted me. *(with a leer)* You still do. *(GIRL turns her whole body away from him, holding out her paper doll as far away from him as possible. He crouches down, reaches around her, snaps the paper doll out of her hand, and places a "shame" sign on her. He stands up and tears off another leg)* Don't blame me for what happened. It was your fault. *(flicks the doll back at her over his shoulder as he exits. Pauses.)* Oh, and by the way, I wouldn't go around telling anybody. You'll just be advertising how easy you are. *(returns to his position)*

One by one each cast member turns, moves toward GIRL, and starts making their hurtful remarks all over again. They form a moving circle around GIRL, talking louder and more intensely. GIRL stands and tries to exit the circle, always staggering away from the harsh words. Finally, holding her ears, she collapses in tears on floor; the talking stops and the circle freezes.

Suddenly GIRL's demeanor changes. She looks up, determined. She walks from actor to actor, snatching back the piece of her paper doll, removing a sign from around her neck, and placing it on the neck of the others with the "blame" side showing.

At last she returns to downstage center and kneels. She attempts to put the doll back together but can't. In tears she holds the pieces heavenward and slowly brings them to her chest and doubles over to the floor. JESUS comes alive and walks through the circle of people to reach GIRL. He kneels next to her and puts his arms over and around her without touching her to show his comfort. He then stands directly behind her, raising his hands and face to heaven in prayer. He then reaches down, places one hand on each of GIRL's shoulders and raises her to a standing position. Simultaneously, GIRL holds up to heaven a completely restored paper doll.

Starting with MOTHER, the other characters come to life and, one at a time, attempt to place their shame and guilt signs back on GIRL. She and JESUS each extend an arm toward the approaching actors, causing them to turn away and freeze.

Finally, Jesus takes GIRL's hand and leads her, weaving in and out of the other actors and then back to downstage center. She lowers herself to the floor with her paper doll and picks up a crayon to color the doll. JESUS takes a step back and lifts his arms and face to heaven in prayer. All the actors except MOTHER remain frozen. MOTHER turns toward JESUS, walks in a circle around him, and then crouches down beside her daughter to admire her paper doll. GIRL looks up at MOTHER and smiles.

Blackout.

END

Living with

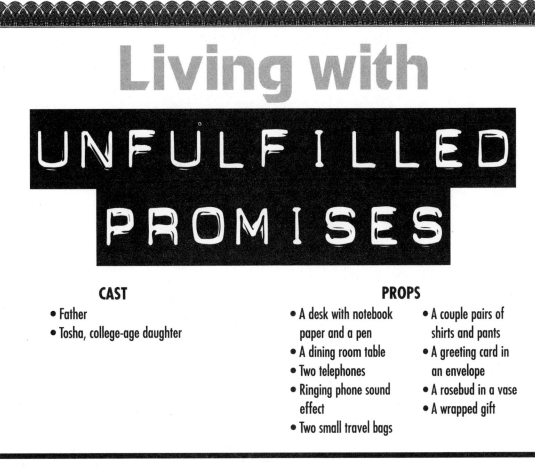

UNFULFILLED PROMISES

CAST

- Father
- Tosha, college-age daughter

PROPS

- A desk with notebook paper and a pen
- A dining room table
- Two telephones
- Ringing phone sound effect
- Two small travel bags
- A couple pairs of shirts and pants
- A greeting card in an envelope
- A rosebud in a vase
- A wrapped gift

Scene 1: On one side of the stage, TOSHA works at her desk in a college dorm room. A phone is within reach. On her bed is an open travel bag and a pile of her clothes. Her FATHER sits on the other side of the stage at the living room table, ready to make a phone call. On the couch is his travel bag, a couple pairs of pants and shirts, a card, and rose bud in a vase.

FATHER: *(picks up the phone and punches in his daughter's number)* 204-523-8971. *(ring)*

TOSHA: *(picks up the phone)* Hello…

FATHER: Hi, honey. How are You?

TOSHA: *(warmly, excited)* Hi, daddy! I'm doing okay. I'm busy with classes and homework, but I'm really excited to see you this weekend!

FATHER: Me, too. I can't believe that my little girl will be eighteen years old.

TOSHA: *(laughing indulgently)* Oh daddy, you're so sentimental.

FATHER: It's just that I miss you, sweetheart. I haven't seen you in so long.

TOSHA: I know, daddy. I miss you, too.

FATHER: So, what time will you be home?

TOSHA: About six o'clock Friday night.

FATHER: Sounds great. I'll be waiting for you. At the right time we'll have a great party together with dinner, cake, and present—the whole shebang! I'm looking forward to us being together the whole time.

TOSHA: Promise?

FATHER: Of course, sweetheart. *(grandly)* Your wish is my command.

TOSHA: I can't wait. *(pause)* I just wish Mom could be there, too.

FATHER: I know, dear. But she'll be with us in her own way.

TOSHA: *(seeming satisfied with that answer)* Six o'clock sharp, then?

FATHER: Six o'clock.

TOSHA: See you Friday.

FATHER: Take care, honey. I'll see you soon.

TOSHA: Bye, Dad.

FATHER: Goodbye, sweetheart.

Both hang up the phone. TOSHA appears excited. She sets aside her work, moves to her travel bag and starts packing. FATHER appears preoccupied. He distractedly packs his bag, sets the card and the rose on the table, and exits. TOSHA finishes packing, closes her bag, and crosses the stage to the table where her father was.

TOSHA: *(joyfully)* Dad! Daddy, I'm home. *(looks around for him)* Daddy? *(the clock chimes six times. Hurt and confused, she exits)*

Here's where the speaker gives the talk (see introduction, page 39). While the audience feels the tension of the broken promise, the speaker suggests that we often feel like Tosha felt when it seems God has not come through on his promises. Usually

our disappointment comes because of misunderstanding of God's ways or timing. Our limited perception of God's purposes obscures the big picture.

Scene 2: The speakers concludes by referring to the card that the father left on the table—Tosha hadn't opened it yet. TOSHA enters, picks up the card, opens it, and mimes reading while FATHER reads it off stage.

FATHER: My dear Tosha. I am so sorry that I cannot be with you tonight on your birthday. Please know that more than anything else in the world I wanted us to be together. I will be home soon and will explain everything then. Please wait for me. Love, Dad.

TOSHA picks up the rose, smells it, holds the card to her heart, and sits at the table to wait for her father to come home. FATHER enters carrying a wrapped gift. TOSHA jumps up and runs to hug him.

TOSHA: Daddy! What happened?

FATHER: Last week I went in for a CAT scan because of some headaches that have been plaguing me for weeks.

TOSHA: What! Oh Daddy, are you okay? You never told me you were having headaches. What did the doctor say? Is it a tumor or something? You should have let me know…

FATHER: *(interrupting)* Whoa, whoa. I can only answer one question at a time.

TOSHA: First the one about whether you're okay.

FATHER: I'm fine. I didn't know that for sure until just this evening. That's why I didn't ask you to come later when we spoke on the phone. I knew you'd ask why and I'd have to explain and you'd be worried and I had no answers. The doctor agreed to meet me after hours today to go over the results with me — he was booked the rest of the day. I wanted to have all that behind us so this weekend we could fully enjoy celebrating your birthday.

TOSHA: *(hugs FATHER)* Oh, Daddy. I love you.

FATHER: Happy birthday, sweetheart. *(hands her the gift)*

END

MANY PARTS

CAST

- Announcer
- Nine busboys
- The prophet
- The two-headed vocalist (two people in one large T-shirt or robe)

PROPS

- Table with two chairs
- Silverware
- A glass
- A large trash can
- Four brooms

• •

ANNOUNCER is alone on the stage, standing in front of a table with silverware, a glass, and other table settings. Two chairs are on either side of the table.

ANNOUNCER: The Apostle Paul described the church as one body made up of many parts. Each part has its own function, which no other member of the body can perform. An eye cannot hear, a foot cannot see, and a nose cannot run...unless you've got a cold. God made each of us with unique gifts and abilities. Of course, sometimes we don't care to be unique. As children and even as adults, we may wish we were more like everybody else.

But think for a minute. Can you imagine what it would be like if we all grew up to be what we wanted as a child? Imagine a world filled with nothing but cowboys, nurses, astronauts, and ballerinas. It simply wouldn't work! Or imagine a world where everyone had the same exact talent, like bussing tables at a restaurant.

ANNOUNCER exits. BUSBOYS enter and all try to clear the table.

ONE: Excuse me, this is my table.

TWO: Oh, no. This is my table.

THREE: You're both wrong! This is my table!

FOUR: What do you mean, it's your table?

FIVE: Exactly! This is my table!

ONE: Is not!

FIVE: Is too!

BUSBOYS ad-lib arguing with each other. PROPHET enters, carrying a trash can containing four brooms. He takes one broom out and bangs it on the ground four times. BUSBOYS freeze.

PROPHET hands out "instruments" to BUSBOYS one by one. Each BUSBOY continues to play the part assigned to him by the prophet, until the rhythms layer together to become a five-part percussion cadence. The notation for the rhythms is on pages 147.

PROPHET hands two spoons to BUSBOY 1, counts off four beats at a moderately fast tempo, and BUSBOY 1 begins playing the spoons on the table.

PROPHET hands BUSBOY 2 a spoon and the glass, which he strikes once on every beat.

PROPHET hands out brooms to BUSBOYS 3, 4, 5, and 6. They walk to the four corners of the stage and, on the PROPHET's cue, begin playing the Broom part—sweep the stage in measures 1, 3, and 4; in measure 2, upend the brooms on beats one and two, and tap the ends of the brooms on the stage for beats three and four.

PROPHET turns the trash can upside down at down stage center. He motions BUSBOY 7 to tilt the bottom of the can out toward the audience and, when cued by the PROPHET, begin playing rhythmically hitting the bottom of the can with his/her fist.

PROPHET turns both chairs to face backstage. The last two BUSBOYS kneel behind the chairs and begin playing their part when PROPHET cues them. (Note: The easiest way to play the chair part is to slap the TOP of the chair for the first three beats and slap the SIDE of the chair for the next two beats. That way they're ready to tap the chair on the stage for the final two beats.)

As all five parts continue to play, PROPHET steps off the stage into the audience to "direct" the strange ensemble. TWO-HEADED VOCALIST enters and sings "Father Abraham" twice, using the following altered lyrics:

Father Abraham had many sons.
  Many sons had Father Abraham.
    I am one of them, and so are you,
      So let's just praise the Lord.
        Right arm, Left arm, Right foot, Left foot, Middle feet,
          Nod your head, Now the other one,
          Turn around, Sit down.

Father Abraham had many sons.
 Many sons had Father Abraham.
  I am one of them, and so are you,
   So let's just praise the Lord.
    Right arm, Left arm, Right foot, Left foot, Middle feet,
     Nod your head, Now the other one,
      Turn around, Sit down.
      Father Abraham.

On the last "Father Abraham," BUSBOYS 3, 4, 5, and 6 flip their brooms over, and BUSBOY 7 turns his trash can upside down over his/her head.

Blackout.

END

Many Parts

John Cosper, Jr.

Spoon Part
Play with Spoons on Table in a Drum Pattern

Glass Part
Play with Spoon Tapping on a Glass

Broom Part
"Sweep" beats indicate sweeping the broom on the stage.
"Tap" beats indicate tapping the broom handle on the stage.

(sweep)   (sweep)   (tap) (tap)   (sweep)   (sweep)   (sweep)   (sweep)

Garbage Can Part
Beats are played by striking the bottom of a Plastic Garbage Can.

Chair Part
"Tap" beats are played by hitting the chair with hands.
"Stomp" beats are played by picking up the chair and banging it on the stage.

(tap)(tap)(tap)(tap)(tap)(stomp) (stomp)

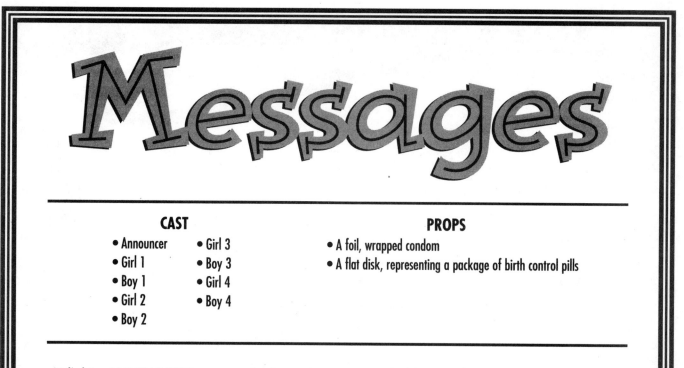

Messages

CAST

- Announcer
- Girl 1
- Boy 1
- Girl 2
- Boy 2
- Girl 3
- Boy 3
- Girl 4
- Boy 4

PROPS

- A foil, wrapped condom
- A flat disk, representing a package of birth control pills

At lights, ANNOUNCER, a causally-dressed young man in his twenties, stands center stage throughout the whole sketch and addresses the audience.

ANNOUNCER: Let's not kid ourselves. You're gonna have sex. And since that's true, you better make sure you're protected. If you're a guy, make sure you use a condom. If you're a girl, use the pill. Or any other effective means of birth control. It's the only way to be safe.

After a beat, GIRL 1 enters and stands at stage right, and BOY 1 enters and stands at stage left. They look straight out over the heads of the audience, expressionless. After a beat or two...

ANNOUNCER: Let's not kid ourselves. You're gonna have sex. And since that's true, you better make sure you're protected. If you're a guy, make sure you use a condom. If you're a girl, use the pill. Or any other effective means of birth control. It's the only way to be safe.

After a beat GIRL 2 enters and stands next to GIRL 1. BOY 2 enters and stands next to BOY 1. They don't acknowledge each other. They stand and look straight out over the heads of the audience. After a beat...

ANNOUNCER: Let's not kid ourselves. You're gonna have sex. And since that's true, you better make sure you're protected. If you're a guy, make sure you use a condom. If you're a girl, use the pill. Or any other effective means of birth control. It's the only way to be safe.

After a beat, BOY 3 and BOY 4 enters to stand next to the other boys. GIRL 3 and GIRL 4 enter and next to the girls already there. After a beat...

ANNOUNCER: Let's not kid ourselves. You're gonna have sex. And since that's true, you better make sure you're protected. If you're a guy, make sure you use a condom. If you're a girl, use the pill. Or any other effective means of birth control. It's the only way to be safe.

BOYS AND GIRLS turn to face each other across the stage and, during the next monolog, they move toward each other, reach out their hands to hold each others' hands, and look at each other. After a beat...

ANNOUNCER: Let's not kid ourselves. You're gonna have sex. And since that's true, you better make sure you're protected. If you're a guy, make sure you use a condom. If you're a girl, use the pill. Or any other effective means of birth control. It's the only way to be safe.

After a beat, the couples slowly hug, and turn slowly upstage. As they turn, they keep one arm around their partner. BOY 1 and GIRL 1 go upstage left. BOY 2 and GIRL 2 go upstage right. BOY 3 and GIRL 3 go downstage left, and BOY 4 and GIRL 4 move downstage right. As they reach their marks, all couples stop.

ANNOUNCER: Let's not kid ourselves. You're gonna have sex. And since that's true, you better make sure you're protected. If you're a guy, make sure you use a condom.

BOYS, except BOY 2, take a condom from their wallets.

ANNOUNCER: If you're a girl, use the pill.

GIRLS, except for GIRL 3, take a disk of pills out of their pockets and hold it up for their partner to see. BOY 2 and GIRL 3 are the only ones to appear nervous and hesitant.

ANNOUNCER: Or any other effective means of birth control. It's the only way to be safe.

After a beat, all couples, with a downstage arm around their partner, slowly sink to the floor, sitting, and draping their arms around each other, hiding each other's faces. They freeze here. Long pause, then—

ANNOUNCER: Let's not kid ourselves. You're gonna have sex. And since that's true, you better make sure you're protected. If you're a guy, make sure you use a condom. If you're a girl, use the pill. Or any other effective means of birth control. It's the only way to be safe.

All couples sink further to floor, starting to lie down together.

ANNOUNCER: Let's not kid ourselves. You're gonna have sex. And since that's true, you better make sure you're protected. If you're a guy, make sure you use a condom. If you're a girl, use the pill. Or any other effective means of birth control.

ANNOUNCER stops as GIRL 3 jumps to her feet, turning from her partner.

GIRL 3: *(quietly)* No. *(more confidently)* No! *(she looks around at the other couples, starts to walk offstage, stops for a moment to look at ANNOUNCER, and then exits. BOY 2 then jumps up and exits, too.)*

ANNOUNCER: *(does not react, resumes)* It's the only way to be safe.

The rest look after GIRL 3 and BOY 2, stunned. They look at each other, rethinking what they are doing. BOY 1 and GIRL 1 slowly get up, straighten themselves, look at ANNOUNCER, and slowly exit, holding hands. BOY 3 and GIRL 2 stand, looking embarrassed, then exit on opposite sides of stage. The last couple, BOY 4 and GIRL 4 look around. GIRL 4 gets up. BOY 4 protests. GIRL 4 waivers, then runs off. BOY 4 sits back down and hugs his knees. After a few beats...

ANNOUNCER: Let's not kid ourselves. *(stands there for several beats, then slowly exits.)*

END

Never Alone

CAST
- Leah, a teen girl who has just been dumped by her boyfriend
- Jesus

PROPS
- Living room furniture — couch, coffee table, lamp
- A teddy bear
- A phone
- An 8x10 picture of a boy

The stage is set like a living room, with a couch, a coffee table, a teddy bear on the couch, and a phone and picture on the table. LEAH walks on from stage left, sobbing. JESUS follows her on. She walks to the picture and picks it up.

LEAH: Oh, Scott. How could you do this to me? Why would you ever want to break up with me? We had the greatest times together! Remember when we went to see <u>Miss Saigon</u>? And what about all those long talks down at the park? And the notes we wrote each other. We were going to make this happen! It was going to be forever! And now…now it's all gone, you fathead! *(slams the picture on the couch. Then, realizing what she's done, she picks it back up and brushes it off, apologetically.)* I didn't mean that! Oh, I'm so sorry! That's no way to win you back. I'm so sorry! *(kisses the picture passionately)*

JESUS: *(grossed out)* Eww!

LEAH: *(puts down the picture and picks up the bear. She shows the bear to the picture.)* Remember him? It's Keanu the Bear. You gave him to me for Christmas, remember? He's the snuggliest guy in the whole world…next to you, of course. I can't tell you the times he's helped me to be brave during thunderstorms. *(hugs bear)* I guess it's a good thing I have him now. I really need someone to love me. The only problem is, when I hug Keanu the Bear, it only makes me think about you! *(throws the bear down and walks to stage left, sobbing)*

I can't believe it. This is the loneliest day of my life! I'm all alone, my boyfriend has dumped me, my friends are all on his side, and nobody cares.

JESUS: I care.

LEAH: Nobody loves me.

JESUS: I do.

LEAH: Nobody will listen to me.

JESUS: I will.

LEAH: Wait a minute! I've got it.

JESUS: *(smiles)* I knew you'd come around.

LEAH: I'll call Tricia!

JESUS: *(caught off guard)* Excuse me?

LEAH: *(picking up the phone and dialing)* I know Tricia! She'll be glad to hear from me. *(holds phone up to her ear, waits, waits,*

83

and waits. Her smile disappears. She hangs up slowly.)

JESUS: She's not home.

LEAH: She's not home. Great. Now who can I talk to?

JESUS whistles and motions to get her attention.

LEAH: *(buries her head in her hands)* Oh, let's face it. I'm an outcast. I'm just cursed to live my life alone! I'm going to be all by myself and I'll die when I'm 97 or something, alone! The little kids in the neighborhood will all be terrified of me. "Look out!" they'll scream. "It's that crazy old witch who lives by herself and eats little children!" Or maybe I'm supposed to go join a convent or something.

JESUS: Or maybe this just wasn't the right one.

LEAH: No, this was my one chance at love, and I blew it. I'm such an idiot. What did I do to turn him off so hard? He must have liked me at some point to give me all the presents he did. *(walks to stage right, toward a window)* Maybe I wasn't appreciative enough and he thought I took him for granted. Once that gets around, I doubt if anybody ever does anything nice for me again.

JESUS: *(has an idea)* I got it! Sunshine!

JESUS aims his finger like a gun at the window and makes a "pow" sound just as LEAH opens up the curtains.

LEAH: Oh, wow! Look at that sun! It's gorgeous. And that blue sky! There's not a cloud anywhere! This would have been the perfect day to go on a picnic with Scott. *(walks away, sobbing.)*

JESUS gives her a "where'd that come from?" look.

LEAH: I'll try to call Tricia again. *(picks up the phone and dials)*

JESUS: She's not home.

LEAH: *(slams down the phone)* She's not home! Oh, I can't stand this! I've got to get out!

JESUS gets another idea. He reaches under the couch and pulls out a dusty Bible.

LEAH: Maybe I oughta go work out at the gym! Or go for a jog in the park! There are a million guys at both places on a day like this, so—

JESUS blows the dust off the Bible, which flies into LEAH's face. She coughs and sneezes.

LEAH: Gee, it's musty in here! Oh well. Anyway, I'll go change, and I'll—

LEAH turns to go. JESUS holds the Bible at her arm's height, and she bumps into it, knocking it on the floor where it falls open.

LEAH: *(looks around, puzzled)* Where did that come from? *(picks up the Bible and reads where it fell open, quickly and without interest—Isaiah 58:9)* "Then you will call and the Lord will answer; you will cry for help, and he will say: (slows down, looking up at JESUS)* 'Here am I.' "

JESUS holds out his hands as if to say, "Here am I."

LEAH: *(looks around and says)* When did you get here?

JESUS give the audience a knowing look.

Blackout.

END

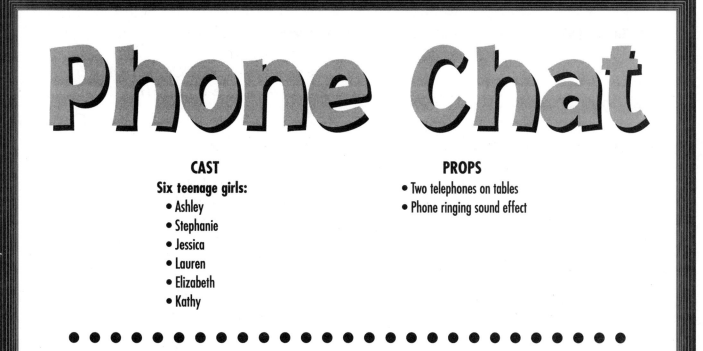

Phone Chat

CAST
Six teenage girls:
- Ashley
- Stephanie
- Jessica
- Lauren
- Elizabeth
- Kathy

PROPS
- Two telephones on tables
- Phone ringing sound effect

● ●

The stage is set up with a phone on either side of the stage. ASHLEY, JESSICA, and ELIZABETH will talk on the phone stage right, and the others will use the stage left phone. ASHLEY enters, picks up the phone, and dials. STEPHANIE enters, answers the other phone.

STEPHANIE: Hello?

ASHLEY: Stephanie? Hi, it's Ashley.

STEPHANIE: Hi, Ashley.

ASHLEY: You're never gonna believe this, but guess who came over last night? Brian Spencer!

STEPHANIE: No way!

ASHLEY: He did! And guess what else? He brought me a puppy dog!

STEPHANIE: Really?

ASHLEY: Yeah! His name's Spike. Isn't that cute?

STEPHANIE: That's so sweet! What did you all do?

ASHLEY: Not a whole lot. Watched TV and played with Spike, mostly. But then, when he was leaving, he kissed me!

STEPHANIE: No way!

ASHLEY: Yes way!

STEPHANIE: Brian Spencer kissed you?

ASHLEY: Uh huh. And Spike got to spend the night in my room!

STEPHANIE: Awww. Brian's so sweet.

ASHLEY: Uh oh. I'm getting beeped by call waiting. I better let you go.

STEPHANIE: Okay. See ya.

The girls hang up. ASHLEY exits. STEPHANIE dials a phone number. JESSICA enters and answers.

JESSICA: Hello?

STEPHANIE: Jessica?

JESSICA: Stephanie! What's going on?

STEPHANIE: Hey, guess what? I just talked to Ashley, and you'll never believe what happened. Brian Spencer kissed her last night!

JESSICA: Shut up! You're lying!

STEPHANIE: No, I'm not! He took his puppy dog Spike over there to spend the night with her!

JESSICA: Well, that is interesting news!

STEPHANIE: Just thought you'd like to know.

JESSICA: Yeah, thanks, Steph. Bye!

The girls hang up. STEPHANIE exits. JESSICA dials a number. LAUREN enters and answers.

LAUREN: Hello?

JESSICA: Lauren! It's Jessica. Guess what I heard? Brian Spencer and some guy named Spike spent the night at Ashley's house last night!

LAUREN: At Ashley's house? No way! You're lying!

JESSICA: I just heard it from Stephanie. And from what she indicated, they were getting more than a little friendly.

LAUREN: Hmmm. Maybe she's not the good little Christian girl she lets on to being at school.

JESSICA: Sure sounds like it, if you ask me. *(looks at watch)* Oh, darn it! I've got to let you go. Oprah's coming on! Catch ya later!

LAUREN: Bye.

The girls hang up. JESSICA exits. LAUREN dials on the phone. ELIZABETH enters and answers.

ELIZABETH: Hello?

LAUREN: Hey, Elizabeth, guess what? I just heard Ashley had a slumber party last night with a couple of boys!

ELIZABETH: What?

LAUREN: Jessica just called and said Brian Spencer and some guy named Spike spent the night over at her house last night!

ELIZABETH: You're kidding!

LAUREN: Just call Jessica if you don't believe me!

ELIZABETH: You don't think she meant Spike Dallas, do you?

LAUREN: Gosh, I hope not! He's got at least five girls pregnant this year! I can't imagine she'd be that stupid!

ELIZABETH: Well, from what you just told me, I'd say there's a lot of things we don't know about Ashley!

LAUREN: You can say that again. I've got to let you go. I just had to tell somebody.

ELIZABETH: Sure. Thanks for calling.

LAUREN: Bye, Elizabeth.

ELIZABETH: Goodbye.

The girls hang up. LAUREN exits. ELIZABETH dials a phone number. KATHY enters and answers.

KATHY: Hello?

ELIZABETH: Kathy, is that you?

KATHY: Hey, Elizabeth. What's up?

ELIZABETH: You are not going to believe what I just heard.

KATHY: Try me.

ELIZABETH: Ashley got knocked up by Spike Dallas!

KATHY: What?

ELIZABETH: Either him or Brian Spencer!

KATHY: Elizabeth, what have you been smoking?

ELIZABETH: I'm serious! They were both over at her house the other night!

KATHY: I can't believe it! Did she want it, or did they force it on her?

ELIZABETH: How should I know? I'm just telling you what I heard from Lauren!

KATHY: Oh my gosh! I better call her and see if she's okay.

ELIZABETH: Uh, I don't know if that's such a good idea.

KATHY: Elizabeth, she may really need a friend right now.

ELIZABETH: Yeah, well, whatever. I'll let you go.

KATHY: Bye.

The girls hang up. ELIZABETH exits. KATHY dials a phone number. ASHLEY enters and answers.

ASHLEY: Hello?

KATHY: Uh, Ashley?

ASHLEY: Hey! Kathy! I've got such exciting news! Did you hear about Brian and Spike?

KATHY: Uhhhh…yeah. I heard all about it.

ASHLEY: Isn't that the sweetest, most romantic thing you've ever heard?

KATHY: Uhhhh…if you say so, Ash.

ASHLEY: *(sighs)* What a night! I can't believe he'd just give it to me like that.

KATHY: Yeah, neither can I. So…do you know if it's a boy or girl yet?

ASHLEY: *(laughs)* Sure I do, silly. It's a boy! How else could I have named it?

KATHY: I don't believe this!

ASHLEY: Yeah, neither can I. I'm just so happy right now!

KATHY: Well, look Ashley, I just wanted to call and let you know I'm here if you need a friend.

ASHLEY: I know that, Kathy.

KATHY: And if there's anything I can do to help, let me know.

ASHLEY: *(puzzled)* Whatever you say, Kathy.

Copyright Youth Specialties, 300 S. Pierce St., El Cajon, CA 92021.

KATHY: So, is Brian going to go to Lamaze class with you?

ASHLEY: *(really puzzled)* Lamaze class?

KATHY: Well, you are going to be prepared for it, aren't you?

ASHLEY: For what?

KATHY: What do you think? Having Brian's baby! You were just talking about naming it and everything!

ASHLEY: *(shocked)* I was what?!?

END

88

Surf City

CAST
- Kyle, teen boy
- P.J., teen girl

PROPS
- Two chairs (folding are easier)
- Two small tables
- TV set, on a stand
- Large remote control, with prop "pull cord" attached to it
- Laundry basket with laundry
- Audiotape of the song "Wipeout" (by the Ventures)
- Sound effect of motor starting, like lawn mower or chainsaw

Set consists of two chairs together, facing downstage, right. A television on a table faces the chairs. There is also a table next to the chairs. The scene opens with KYLE entering stage left, dressed in T-shirt and jeans.

KYLE: *(big yawn)* Oh, man, what a day... *(wanders over to the chairs, consults watch)* Let's see, I haven't watched any TV in about *(counts silently on his fingers)* ...20 minutes. Wonder what's on? *(he goes to TV, pretending to turn it on, then sits down on one of the chairs and leans back)* Cool! I love this show! "Boys and Their Toys"...

KYLE sits and watches for a beat or two, then P.J. enters from stage left. She's dressed casually and carries a load of laundry. She sees KYLE, but can't see what's on the TV yet. Sets the laundry down on table.

P.J.: What's the matter, Kyle? Afraid the TV was cooling off too much? I'm SO sure I have to do chores while you watch TV!

KYLE: *(doesn't take eyes from TV)* I told mom that I needed to uh, catch this uh, PBS after-school special on, uh...uh...er...

P.J.: Being a dork?

89

KYLE: Ohhh. Ouch. *(referring to the tube)* It's legit. I'm learning already.

P.J.: *(starts folding the laundry, sarcastic tone)* Oh, excuse me, I didn't realize you were cramming for your Ph.D. *(heads towards the TV)* Hmmmm. Let's just see which lecture on rocket science you're watching.

KYLE: *(jumps up nervously, runs to TV, and tries to hide the screen from her view)* Uh, you don't want to watch this, it's just some lecture on uh...global warming...yeah...

P.J.: Oh, really? *(pushing him back to his chair)* I've always wanted to know more about the environment.

KYLE looks nervously off to side while P.J. watches for a few beats.

P.J.: *(dripping with sarcasm)* Ahhh, I see. You must have turned on some PBS documentary about monster truck rallies! I bet those trucks really do warm up the planet with all that exhaust. And they are saving room in our landfills by crushing those cars like that. Oh, and those drivers do look like real environmental crusaders. *(angry)* I'm gonna tell Mom you...

KYLE: *(interrupts)* Okay, okay, quiet! I just wanted to watch something entertaining, so sue me. Look, why don't you sit down and we can watch something that we both like. Mom says we should try to get along better, anyway.

P.J.: Hmmm. Well, I was in the middle of having a life. Guess five minutes won't matter...if we don't have to watch the rest of this tribute to boyhood. *(sits next to him)*

KYLE: Okay, okay... *(looks around on the floor)* Have you seen the remote? *(panics)* Where's the remote?! Where is it? I...oh yeah, I remember where it is... *(goes to table, opens drawer, and pulls out a remote control that has a long cord wrapped around it, with a wooden handle at the end of the cord. He holds it up with satisfaction.)* Yeah, just got this baby at the hardware store...it's one of those new 10 horsepower jobs, with a pull start! *(he pulls cord off like he's starting an engine. Chain saw motor sound effect comes up for a beat)* Let's see what she do!

KYLE points the remote at the TV and starts to slowly change from channel to channel, making a big motion with his thumb. The song "Wipeout" starts as KYLE starts moving his thumb faster and faster, "zapping" the TV. He then stands up and pretends to start surfing, then moves around the set, changing channels from behind his back, between his legs, pulling remote out of an imaginary holster, using his chin, ear, nose to change channels, throwing it up in the air and catching it and changing the channel, holding up a hand mirror, turning his back on the TV and using the mirror to see the TV behind him, etc. Should be played BIG. During this, P.J. stares at the TV, trying to watch, then does a slow burn. Finally, her frustration boils over.

P.J.: *STOP IT!*

The music stops cold as KYLE freezes in a final "zapping" position.

KYLE: What?

P.J.: You do this ALL the time! You change the channels so fast, I can't tell if the show's any good or not!

KYLE: Oh, it's easy to tell! *(counts on his fingers)* Any time you see an orchestra...or a weather map...or an episode of "The Love Boat" or someone with a microphone standing in an audience, or someone saying, "This beautiful diamond ring was 2 million dollars...your TV shopper price...11 bucks"...that's when you know it's time to surf right on by.

P.J.: Well, maybe I want to see some of those programs.

KYLE: *(whines)* Look, I...I just can't help it. I have to see what's on all the other channels. *(cuddles remote to his chest, away from her)* It's a guy thing.

P.J.: Okay, I'll make you a deal. I won't tell Mom what you're up to IF we just watch something for 10 seconds before you flip it? Just 10 seconds?

KYLE: *(leery)* Welllll...I guess we can try it. *(points the remote again and pushes once. Then, out of the side of his mouth, he starts counting)* One one thousand, two one thousand, three one thousand, *(he starts counting faster and faster until)* TEN ONE THOUSAND! *(he points the remote and starts flipping again. "Wipeout" music comes up for a second as he jumps around changing channels again.)*

P.J.: *(going back to her laundry)* MOMMMMM!!

KYLE: All right! *(points remote at the TV)* There. The 24-hour Chick Channel. All chick stuff, all the time.

P.J.: You're SO lame.

KYLE: Ha. Look at this commercial! I hate this one! It's soooooo stupid! They claim that by adding their little gizmo-thing-deal to your car's engine, that it'll run like a hundred times better than it does now. A hundred times! Like something that small would make such a big difference. Like, how stupid do they think we are?

P.J. starts to respond, but KYLE holds up his hand.

KYLE: Never mind.

After a beat, P.J. puts down the laundry and goes to KYLE.

P.J.: *(quieter)* Hey, did you hear Mom and Dad fighting last night?

KYLE: Huh?

P.J.: Hello? Mom and Dad fighting?

KYLE: Yeah. And...?

P.J.: Dad had that stupid remote going a hundred miles an hour like you do and Mom was yelling at him.

KYLE: The teacher and the pupil.

P.J.: It wasn't funny. They got real mad. She said *(taking the remote)* this thing...this little thing...was making too much trouble. It was making too much of a big difference in their marriage.

KYLE: Huh? *(gesturing at remote)* This thing?

P.J.: Yeah. She said they never talk or stuff any more. Because of this little thing. Then they kept fighting, and I went to bed.

KYLE: Oh, they always fight.

P.J.: Not like this. I...never mind. You don't care, anyway. *(resumes her laundry duties)*

After several beats, KYLE takes the remote, studies it, then the tube, and points it to the tube.

KYLE: Guess it can be off for a while, huh?

P.J.: *(curtly)* Fine.

KYLE: Hey, uh, P.J., ya wanna go to the mall? Justin and those guys said they'd be there.

P.J.: You never invite me out with your friends.

KYLE: Maybe I should...more. I don't know. Never mind. *(getting up)*

P.J.: No, wait. Okay, sure. Uh, thanks. You know?

KYLE: Yeah, 'kay. Doesn't mean I like you more or anything.

P.J.: *(smiling)* Right. Me neither.

They both get up, and MANDIE exits stage right. KYLE goes to put down the remote, but can't seem to let go of it. He tries to "pry" it from his hand, and he won't let go. He turns on the TV and the music comes up again for a beat. P.J. re-enters and sees what's happening.

P.J.: EXCUSE me?!

KYLE: *(startled, throwing remote up in air, music stops cold)* Just, ah, checking the Weather Channel before we go out. Yeah, that's it!

P.J. exits.

KYLE: *(yelling after her as he starts to exit)* I was checking the weather out at the mall! Really! Don't tell...

P.J.: *(offstage)* MOMMMM!

KYLE throws his hands up and exits.

END

Copyright Youth Specialties, 300 S. Pierce St., El Cajon, CA 92021.

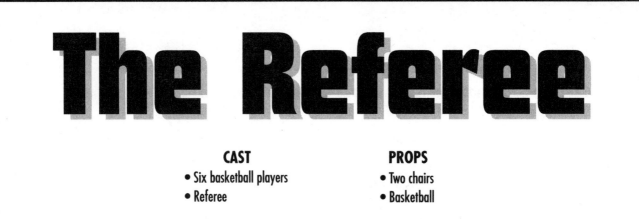

The Referee

CAST	**PROPS**
• Six basketball players	• Two chairs
• Referee	• Basketball

The scene
On the two chairs at opposite ends of the stage, two people stand, forming a basketball hoop with their arms. THE PLAYERS begin to warm up for a game. They ad lib chatter, laughing, pumping each other up, and talking basketball. PLAYER 1 suggests they play a game. They quickly pick sides and begin to play. They are laughing, having a lot of fun, and enjoying each other's company.

After about minute, THE REFEREE wanders onto the scene. He aggressively blows the whistle and waves his arms to stop the action.

PLAYER 1: Hey! What're you doing? We're trying to play a game here.

REFEREE: You can't play a game yet. You're missing the most important ingredient...me!

PLAYER 2: What do we need you for? We've got a ball. We've got a court. And we've got two good teams. What else do we need?

REFEREE: You need a good whistle blower to protect the purity of the game. *(grabs the ball, hands it to PLAYER 2 , and points to one of the baskets)* Now quit stalling. It's your ball, going this way.

THE PLAYERS shrug, look at each other, and begin to play. THE REFEREE intensely follows the action and quickly makes his first call with a lot of authority. THE PLAYERS look a little surprised, but follow his command. The game continues. THE REFEREE is very picky and obnoxious to the point that the group can't play for more than a few seconds without the ref blowing the whistle. THE PLAYERS lose the enjoyment of the game and get frustrated. After about the fifth call, PLAYER 4 stops the ball and confronts the ref.

PLAYER 4: Foul? C'mon. This is no fun!

REFEREE: *(blows whistle)* That's a technical foul on the short kid! *(signals technical foul)*

PLAYER 3: What? You gotta be crazy!

REFEREE, PLAYER 3, and a couple other players begin to argue.

PLAYER 1: Look, you guys, this just isn't working out at all. The game is being ruined. This is a great sport, but we're not even able to enjoy it right now.

PLAYER 4: Yeah, we're so worried about the rules, we've lost the freedom to play the game and just enjoy it.

PLAYER 1: You're right. *(to REFEREE)* Give me the ball. You're outta here. Get lost. *(to the group)* I've got an idea. We all know the rules. Let's play without a referee and make our own calls. Let's let the spirit of the game guide our play. If we're completely honest with each other, I think it will work.

All agree.

PLAYER 4: Sounds like a great idea. If one of us travels or double dribbles, we'll call it ourselves.

PLAYER 5: Yeah, and if I foul one of you, I'll call it too.

The group begins play again, and one of the players makes a great play to score.

PLAYER 1: *(throws up his arms in celebration)* I love this game!

The whistle blows and the action freezes.

NARRATOR: "It is for freedom that Christ has set us free. Stand firm then and do not let yourselves be weighted down by the saddle of slavery. Those of you who are trying to be justified by following the rules have been alienated from Christ; you have fallen away from grace. Instead, we (by faith) eagerly await, through the Spirit, the righteousness for which we hope. You were playing a good game. Who interrupted you and kept you from obeying the truth? Such persuasion does not come from above. For in Christ Jesus the only thing that counts is faith expressing itself through love." Galatians 5:1-12, paraphrased.

END

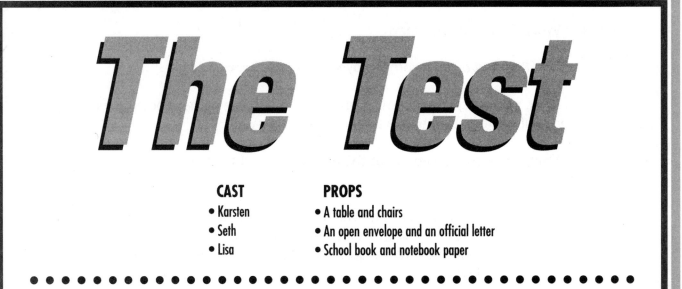

The Test

CAST
- Karsten
- Seth
- Lisa

PROPS
- A table and chairs
- An open envelope and an official letter
- School book and notebook paper

● ●

SETH sits at a table doing homework. KARSTEN struts in, smiling at a letter he's carrying. He slides it in front of SETH.

SETH: *(picking up the letter)* What's this?

KARSTEN: Nothin' much. Something from the University of Miami!

SETH: Yeah? What's it say?

KARSTEN: It say that you're in the same room as the next quarterback for the mighty Miami Hurricanes!

SETH: Dude! You've been offered a scholarship to Miami?

KARSTEN: *(pulling out a chair, turning it around, and sitting backwards on it)* Yeah. Coach McDonald nearly choked on his whistle when I showed him.

SETH: So, are you going to take it?

KARSTEN: Is the sky blue? Heck yeah, I'm going to take it!

SETH: Cool!

KARSTEN: Yeah, I figure I'll start as a freshman, rack up a few championship rings, break every existing Miami record by the time I'm a junior, win a Heisman trophy or two, then skip my final season and cut straight to the big show—the NFL!

SETH: Whoa! Man, you've got it made!

KARSTEN: No kidding!

SETH: So did you tell Carrie yet?

KARSTEN: Not yet. I know she's gonna be excited, though.

Copyright Youth Specialties, 300 S. Pierce St., El Cajon, CA 92021.

SETH: Why wouldn't she? How often does a girl go out with a future All-American!

KARSTEN: Nothing could ruin my day right now. Life just doesn't get any better than this.

LISA enters hurriedly, walks to the table.

LISA: Hi, Seth.

KARSTEN: Hi, Lisa. What's up?

LISA: *(looks nervously at KARSTEN)* I need to talk to you. *(pointedly)* Alone.

SETH shrugs, stands up and walks out. LISA sits down.

KARSTEN: *(clueless about the tension in the room)* I was just showing Seth my national letter of intent to play football at the University of Miami. I got a football scholarship to Miami!

LISA: *(unenthused)* Swell.

KARSTEN: *(sarcastic)* Please, try to contain your excitement.

LISA: I have something to tell you…about Carrie.

KARSTEN: What about her?

LISA: Well, she kind of took a test yesterday.

KARSTEN: Oh yeah? Like, what, SAT? ACT?

LISA: No, EPT.

KARSTEN: *(doesn't realize EPT is a pregnancy test)* Cool. How'd she do?

LISA: Uhhh, I guess you could say she…passed.

KARSTEN: She's good. *(starts to stand up from the chair)* So I'll give her a call. I guess congratulations are in order.

LISA: *(cocks an eyebrow)* Well, I guess so, if you mean, "Congratulations, you're going to be a father."

KARSTEN freezes in shock, collapses back onto his chair. Blackout.

END

Voices

CAST
- Laura, teenage girl considering suicide
- Death
- Laura's mom (offstage voice)
- Sandy, Kelly and David, Laura's friends (offstage voices)
- Christine, Laura's 5-year-old sister (offstage voice)
- Other voices: teacher, boy, three girls
- Jesus

● ●

Lights are out. Offstage voices start a volley of negative statements.

TEACHER: Laura, I'm so disappointed in you.

GIRL 1: Laura, what do you think you're doing?

BOY: You're so pathetic. How could I have ever thought I loved you?

GIRL 2: Some friend you are!

BOY: *(annoyed and disgusted)* Oh, Laura!

GIRL 3: Darn it, Laura, cut it out!

GIRL 2: Leave me alone!

BOY: You're always moping. It's like nothing good ever happens to you!

TEACHER: Laura!

GIRL 1: Go away!

GIRL 3: Don't ever speak to me again!

GIRL 2: *(angry)* Oh, Laura.

BOY: Laura!

GIRL 1: Laura!

Lights up. LAURA is alone stage right, bent over on her knees. DEATH walks in from stage left, slowly.

DEATH: *(dark and seductive)* Nobody loves you. Nobody cares. Everyone around you has something going for them. But not you. You can't sing. You're incredibly uncoordinated. You're not very intelligent. There's nothing remarkable about you. No one would even notice if you were suddenly gone.

LAURA slowly gets up and walks toward DEATH.

DEATH: Yes, come to me. I do want you. No one's going to miss you. It'll be a relief to them to have you out of the way.

When MOM speaks, DEATH loses its concentration. LAURA gets scared, turns away from DEATH, and walks back toward stage right.

MOM: *(desperate, crying loudly)* Oh, Laura! Laura, why did you do this? You were my baby. I love you SO MUCH!

DEATH: Don't listen to her! *(LAURA freezes)* She doesn't really love you! She may pretend, but I see what's inside her mind. The moment she finds out you're thinking about ending it all, she'll have you locked up! Is that what you want?

LAURA shakes her head. She turns back to DEATH and starts moving toward him again.

DEATH: Yes, she won't miss you. She has a career to worry about. In six months she'll have forgotten about you completely.

SANDY: *(distressed, crying)* Why didn't you come to me? Didn't our friendship mean anything to you? I loved you, Laura. I said I'd always be there for you. Why didn't you come?

LAURA turns away from DEATH again.

DEATH: You're too smart to fall for that line. Do you really think anyone would drop everything for you? She's got a life, you know. Why would she want to sit and listen to you whine!

DAVID: *(sadly)* What were you thinking? Did you really think that no one cared? That no one would listen?

LAURA becomes frantic, turning back and forth as each voice speaks.

DEATH: You can't run to him—not after the way you broke his heart. He's much better off without you.

KELLY: *(gently)* We promised to look out for each other, remember. You were always there for me. Did you think I wouldn't do the same for you?

DEATH: Empty promises? Haven't you hurt enough for three lifetimes? Why don't you just leave it all behind? It would be such a relief to just let go of your miserable little life.

CHRISTINE: *(urgent)* Laura? Why did you leave us? Why did you go away?

LAURA turns decisively away from DEATH. Swiftly he moves toward her.

DEATH: *(reprovingly)* Do you mean to say you'd listen to a 5-year-old over your own heart?

LAURA freezes, her back to DEATH, as he continues to approach her.

DEATH: Going away is the more mature choice. You can't keep disappointing and hurting the people you care about. What kind of an example are you to a 5-year-old girl? If you love her at all, you'll leave before she finds out what you did to "prove" your love to your last boyfriend.

LAURA winces at his comments. She puts her head in her hands and starts to cry. CHRISTINE sings "Jesus Loves Me." LAURA lifts her face from her hands and listens.

DEATH: *(faster; less smug)* You're living in a world full of sinners. Friends who betray you. Parents who deceive you. Teachers who don't care. *(points at her accusingly)* And you're the worst!

LAURA: *(screaming, frightened)* No!

DEATH: Don't run from me, Laura. There's no turning back!

LAURA: Oh, God, please help me!

At the mention of God, DEATH whirls and runs off. LAURA collapses to her knees in tears.

LAURA: *(whispers)* Help me, Jesus. Please help me.

CHRISTINE continues to sing. JESUS enters from stage right. Reaching down to gently grasp her shoulders, he helps her to her feet, then picks her up in his arms, and carries her off stage. The lights go down while CHRISTINE finishes her song. Blackout.

END

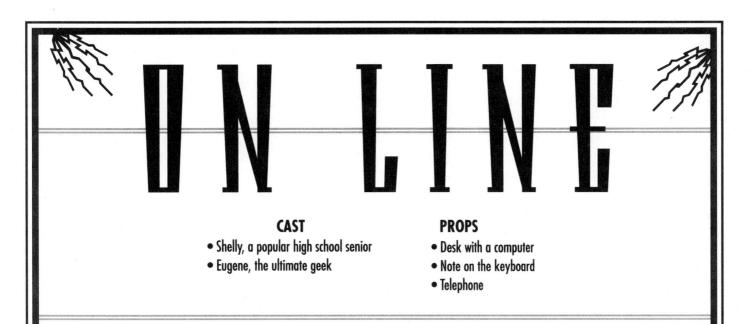

ON LINE

CAST
- Shelly, a popular high school senior
- Eugene, the ultimate geek

PROPS
- Desk with a computer
- Note on the keyboard
- Telephone

SHELLY is pacing in her den talking on the telephone. A computer is set up on a desk stage left with a note on top.

SHELLY: Hey, Kristin? It's Shelly. You called?…She called practice? Tonight? As if I didn't have enough to do!…Well, I was supposed to go to the movies with Josh, but before I can do that, I have to finish my Internet research project. And I can't do my research project because the computer's not working right. What's even worse, my dad's out of town. So guess who I had to call to get the computer fixed?

EUGENE enters. SHELLY has her back turned to him.

EUGENE: Hey there, hot stuff! How's it shakin'?

SHELLY: *(startled)* Don't ever do that to me, Eugene! You almost gave me a heart attack!

EUGENE: Sorry.

SHELLY: The computer's over there. Dad left you a note on the keyboard. *(on phone)* I'm sorry, Kristin, Eugene snuck up on me.

EUGENE: Wow, it's the *MegaMac PC 6000! 128 megs of RAM, a 32x variable speed CD ROM drive, and the XQ-32-ZS-80000 quadlink modem!* **(substitute the latest and best computer set up)**

EUGENE goes to the computer and reads the note.

SHELLY: Hmmm? Oh, Eugene's just lusting over my dad's computer…No, I don't know a thing about 'em, either…Yeah, I guess I'll see you at practice…I don't know. I'm not even sure why I want to do it any more. Mom got me into cheerleading when my brothers played PeeWee football, and I've been stuck ever since.

EUGENE: *(working on the computer)* All right. We have the top of the line modem, which is not connecting up properly to the local web server.

SHELLY: Eugene, I'm on the phone. Do you mind?

EUGENE: No, no, go right ahead. The computer's on a separate line.

SHELLY: I meant could you please keep it down?

EUGENE: Sorry.

EUGENE goes back to work on the back of the computer.

SHELLY: Sorry, Kristin. Where was I?…Oh, cheerleading. I've been offered a full ride scholarship to cheer for Vanderbilt in Nashville…Room and board, tuition, books, everything! Mom really wants me to take it…Well, it would be great if I wanted to cheer for four more years, but I don't.

EUGENE: *(working on the computer)* Okay, if that's not working, what other options do I have?

SHELLY: Dad's been trying to talk me into engineering for years. He'd love to see his little girl follow in his footsteps…I applied to MIT and Purdue, and I got accepted both places.

EUGENE: *(to SHELLY)* You got accepted to MIT? They won't even return my calls!

SHELLY: Was I talking to you?

EUGENE: Sorry.

SHELLY: Sorry, Kristin. Anyway, in addition to all that, Miss Taylor's arranged a vocal audition with the Philadelphia Conservatory…Yes, the Conservatory!…I know, that would be really cool, too. But then there's our children's minister who wants me to go to Bible college.

EUGENE: *(working on the computer)* All the options are hooked in. *(scratches head)* So, what exactly is the problem?

SHELLY: I don't know what to do! I know I could be good at any one of those, but I'm not sure which one will make me the most happy! The deadline to accept or reject my scholarships is two weeks away, and I have no clue how I'm gonna decide which one to accept! Who do I listen to? My mom, my dad, Miss Taylor…And what about Josh? He wants me to go to State so we can be together.

EUGENE: *(working on the computer)* So, we've got the fax line here, the office line here, the bedroom line here, another fax line here, and then the modem.

SHELLY: I know God has a wonderful plan for my life, and there's got to be a way to figure out what that is, but how will I find it?

EUGENE: *(working on the computer)* Aha! I've found the problem!

SHELLY: *(to EUGENE)* Will you please keep it down?

EUGENE: *(ignores her)* It's so simple, it's right in front of my face! All these alternate sources are cluttering the line of communication! Once you disconnect the other sources, information can flow unobstructed from the main server. *(SHELLY freezes, looks up, then slowly turns to EUGENE)*

SHELLY: What did you just say?

EUGENE: I said, if you unhook all the other sources, information can flow unobstructed from the main server to you.

SHELLY: *(looks hard at EUGENE, then after a beat)* Yeah…*(to Kristin)* I'll call you back.

SHELLY hangs up and walks to EUGENE.

EUGENE: *(fearful)* What? I'm…I'm sorry I was talking…I didn't mean to…please don't hit me!

SHELLY lurches forward, teasing like she's going to hit EUGENE, then hugs him.

SHELLY: Thanks.

EUGENE: For what?

SHELLY: For helping me solve my problems.

EUGENE: The computer's not fixed yet.

SHELLY: No. About college. About my life. Like you said, too many alternate sources in my life are blocking me from hearing from the main source. I've missed out hearing God.

EUGENE: You got all that from me talking to myself? Crazy.

SHELLY: Eugene, I've had the hardest time figuring out what to do about school, and now I know why. I need God's help in these decisions. *(she hugs EUGENE again)* How can I ever thank you enough?

EUGENE: Uh, will you go to the prom with me?

SHELLY: Not a chance.

EUGENE: *(dejected)* Oh.

SHELLY: But I'll get you some ice cream.

EUGENE: Well…okay.

SHELLY takes EUGENE by the arm. They walk out slowly.

END

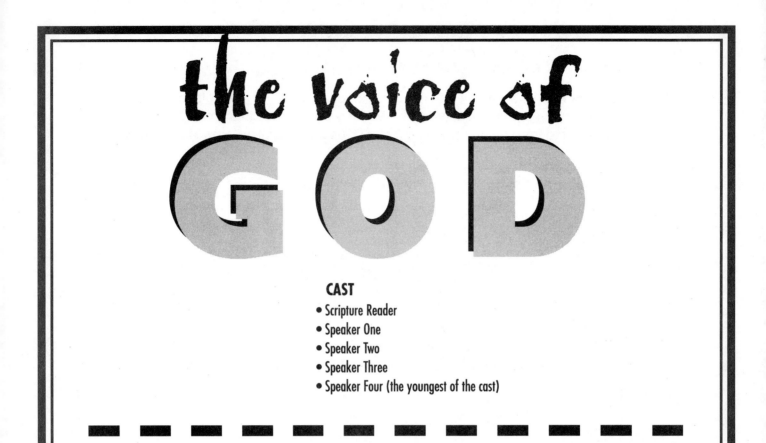

the voice of GOD

CAST
- Scripture Reader
- Speaker One
- Speaker Two
- Speaker Three
- Speaker Four (the youngest of the cast)

■ ■ ■ ■ ■ ■ ■ ■ ■ ■ ■

Every three to five minutes during the worship service, an offstage, miked voice representing the voice of God calls the name of the various people leading the morning worship.

While the associate pastor is making the announcements, for instance, the voice calls her or his name. The voice calls the name of a deacon who's taking the offering, a musician who's in the middle of accompanying a song, the pastor leading the morning prayer. These leaders, clued in ahead of time, act completely oblivious to the voice at all times.

Finally, as the Scripture is being read just before the sermon, SPEAKER ONE stands and interrupts the Scripture reader.

ONE: Hey, hold on a second! Is it just me, or is something going on here that we're not paying attention to?

READER: *(indignantly)* _____ , sit down! We're right in the middle of a church
(name of speaker one)
service. What are you doing?

ONE: No, the question is, What are <u>you</u> doing?

READER: What are you talking about? I'm reading the Bible, if you don't mind.

ONE: Well, maybe you should stop talking and listen. Ever since we started this morning's service, there's been a voice calling out your name and _____'s name and
(name of pastor)
_____'s names.
(names of others who were called)

READER: A voice? Are you nuts?

TWO: *(standing up)* Yeah, a voice. I heard it, too! It was calling out your names, just like he said.

READER: Both of you, sit down! You're interrupting the flow of worship.

ONE: I'm not going to sit down until we find out what's going on here today.

TWO: You know what I think? I think it was the voice of God, and everyone was too busy leading the service to listen.

ONE: Yeah. You're supposed to be leading us to worship God, but when God calls you, you ignore him.

READER: I think not. If God were actually to call, the worship leaders would be the ones to hear God's voice.

THREE: *(standing)* Well, I heard it, too. *(addressing the congregation)* Did anyone else hear God calling this morning?

READER: Oh, this is ridiculous!

FOUR: I may be younger than most everybody else here, but I heard God this morning, too.

ONE: You know what I think?

READER: No, what do you think?

ONE: I think _____'s right. Even in church we can get so intent on doing our
(name of SPEAKER TWO)
thing that we don't hear God's voice when he calls.

VOICE: *(calls out the reader's name and the church's name)*

READER: What was that?!

THREE: That was it! That was the voice!

ONE: *(looking up)* We're here, Lord. We're listening.

READER: *(incredulously)* Lord, is that really you?

VOICE: Why does my voice surprise you? I speak to you quite often.

READER: If you say so, Lord. I guess I'm a little slow to hear you. What do you want us to do?

VOICE: I want you to open your ears and open your hearts. I am not silent. Slow down. Begin to listen. Hear my voice and be willing to follow and obey me.

READER: Speak to us, Lord. We're ready to listen.

END

The Waiter

CAST
- Waiter
- Boss (offstage voice)
- Six customers, stationed throughout the audience
- Jesus (offstage voice)

PROPS
- Apron, white shirt and tie for waiter
- An order pad, pen, serving tray and towel

Scene: WAITER enters, puts on his apron, and gathers his pad, pen, towel, tray as he talks with the BOSS.

BOSS: You're late again. That makes three times this week. What's your excuse this time?

WAITER: Sorry, I got caught in traffic.

WAITER moves into the audience to the six people who have been prepped to place an order with the waiter. The WAITER writes down each order as it is given.

CUSTOMER 1: I'm really hungry. Could I talk you out of a burger and fries? A kid's meal will do.

CUSTOMER 2: Water is all I need right now. A tall, cold glass of water.

CUSTOMER 3: I'm a stranger in town and I have no place to sleep tonight. I don't know anybody else to ask, so could you tell me where I might find a bed for the night?

WAITER: I'm sorry, but that's not exactly the kind of order we fill at this restaurant. I'm sure there's a downtown mission that would be able to help you out. Excuse me. *(moves on to the customer 4)*

CUSTOMER 4: Thanks for coming to take my order. I'm running a slight fever and I've had this nagging headache for several days. It's getting so I can't easily take care of myself. I'd like to request someone to come take care of me for a while.

WAITER: I don't know why you're telling me this. I take orders from our preprinted menu. We sell meals here, not medical assistance. Excuse me. *(moves on to customer 5)*

CUSTOMER 5: I know it's not the deep winter, but even so, sleeping outside at night gives my old bones a chill. I need some long underwear and a good coat.

WAITER: Look, I don't know if someone changed the sign in the window or what, but this is a restaurant. A place to buy food. Try the thrift shop down the street for clothes. Please excuse me. *(becomes agitated as he moves to customer 6)*

CUSTOMER 6: This is my last night of freedom for a long time. My jail sentence begins tomorrow. I'm feeling lonely and depressed already. Could you see your way to visit me in jail?

WAITER: Visit you in… What is going on here? My job is waiting tables, not playing confessor to jailbirds. *(mutters as he makes his way back to the stage area)* What kind of Twilight Zone did I walk into tonight? Is this the boss's way of getting to me about being late? *(looks around from the stage to see if any other customers need attention, and see a new customer at the back of the auditorium. The new customer is an offstage voice.)* Oh no, another customer.

WAITER: I almost hate to ask, but is there anything I can get for you?

JESUS: No, nothing for me, thanks. But I was wondering, is there anything I could get for you?

WAITER: Yeah, some Tylenol.

JESUS: Been a rough day, huh?

WAITER: I'll say. This whole serving profession isn't all it's cracked up to be. Can you believe these people? This is a restaurant, for crying out loud, not a Goodwill outlet or a pharmacy. I mean, I can appreciate that people have problems—I have my headache, but I don't go ask the short order cook for a CAT scan. There are limits to what I can do.

JESUS: It's a good thing there were no limits on what I was willing to give for you.

WAITER: What do you mean?

JESUS: I gave everything for you when I died and then rose again. I did it so you could live.

WAITER: Jesus? Oh, man, I didn't recognize you! I don't believe this…Jesus Christ, right here in my restaurant. Seriously, what can I get for you. It's on the house. Anything at all. We've got a really great special—catch of the day and…

JESUS: Do you really want to serve me?

WAITER: It would be an honor. Please, let me get your something.

JESUS: If you want to serve me...serve them. *(gestures to the audience)*

WAITER: *(looks to audience)* Them?

JESUS: Yes. Whatever you do to the least of these people, you do it to me. When you serve them, you serve me. It's that straight across. If someone is hungry and you feed her, you feed me. When you give someone a glass of water in my name, you're giving it to me. When you welcome strangers into your home, when you clothe those without clothes, when you visit the lonely and imprisoned, when you help those who can't help themselves—whatever you do for the least of these my brothers, you do for me.

WAITER: And if I ignore them?

JESUS: You're ignoring me.

WAITER: Are you serious?

JESUS: Yes...very.

WAITER: Will you excuse me for a moment. I have some work to do. *(gathers props and heads back into the audience)*

READER: "But because of his great love for us, God, who is rich in mercy, made us alive with Christ even when we were dead in transgressions—it is by grace you have been saved. And God raised us up with Christ and seated us with him in the heavenly realms in Christ Jesus, in order that in the coming ages he might show the incomparable riches of his grace, expressed in his kindness to us in Christ Jesus. For it is by grace you have been saved, through faith — and this not from yourselves, it is the gift of God — not by works, so that no one can boast. For we are God's workmanship, created in Christ Jesus to do good works, which God prepared in advance for us to do." *(Ephesians 2:4-10)*

END

TV
TAKEOFFS

In a TV world of talk shows and sitcoms, sketches based on TV shows always kick off lively discussions. Since all these scripts are also humorous, they're great as openers at camps and conferences, too.

SEVEN DEADLY SINS

The "Seinfeld" cast may have done their last season, but the spirit of Seinfeld lives on in this series of seven sketches on pages 113-137 (envy, sloth, anger, greed gluttony, pride, lust). Without apologies, the characters in these sketches are patterned after the cast of "Seinfeld" (a classic show, even if it lacks good theology). The cast should purposely imitate the personalities of George, Jerry, Kramer, and Elaine.

These humorous scripts wouldn't substitute as a lesson. They're best used, one per week, to spark a lesson or a discussion on one of the seven deadly sins. *Scott Davis*

FUSSY 'BOUT YOUR FRIENDS
GAME SHOW FOR THE SOCIALLY ACCEPTABLE

Followers of Christ don't get to choose their traveling companions on the journey of faith—Jesus chooses. Like his original disciples, we can wind up part of a motley crew. The three contestants in this game show, however, are Christians looking to win socially acceptable relationships and reputations. But the "Whammies" dash their hopes on the brink of "success."

To turn the sketch into a discussion starter, conclude by reading Mark 2:13-17 or selected verses from James 1 and 2. Lead the group to recognize that Christians are off the mark if we limit our friendships to the up and coming, excluding the different or needy from our circle of friends. The script is on page 138.

- **Staging the skit**
The host stands behind a podium on one side of the stage, and the three contestants stand behind smaller podiums on the other side. In the middle of the stage hangs the giant game board sheet. Beside the sheet is a six-inch diameter, red button that contestants will hit to stop the "spin" on the game board. You'll also need a bell to ring for a winning spin and a buzzer to sound for a losing spin.

To simulate an electronic game board, place two assistants holding flashlights behind the sheet. When the host says to starts the spin, the assistants move the lights behind the sheet and make big game board noises.

- **Making the major prop**

On a queen-size, white bed sheet, use extra fat, permanent markers to draw a game board like this:.

Decorate the game board with colored markers and simple drawings. Instead of merely writing "Ivory," for instance, write it inside a drawing of a bar of soap. The impact of the skit is worth the effort you'll put into making the show props. You could even share it with First Church across town.

- **Creating the prize board**
Using poster board, an overhead projector, or slides (if you have the technology), display three columns with a contestant's name at the top of each. As they win friendship prizes, the beautiful assistant records the winnings as in the sample below.
Scott Davis

THE PLAYER
1 CORINTHIANS 9:25; 1 TIMOTHY 4:8

We all know Christians who never pick up their Bible, never participate in group activities or ministry opportunities, never practice their faith, but show up to church every once in a while if they have nothing better to do. The sketch on page 144 is just zany enough to get kids wondering how such a person could actually consider themselves to be Christian.

Follow the skit with a spiritual workout. Do some Bible calisthenics (remember "sword drills"), exercise their faith by leading them into group prayer, invite them to get stronger during the week with a spiritual discipline of daily prayer, a day of fasting and prayer, daily Bible reading, or taking a Sabbath. *Teresa McCasland*

TOOL TIME RESTORATION GOSPEL

This takeoff on the popular TV show "Home Improvement" presents the gospel according to Wilson. "Hi-de-ho, neighbor!" Then Tim the Toolman Taylor's wife, Jill, lays out the plan of salvation so that even Tim gets it. You might find that Tim's response to the message of salvation in Jesus prompts eternally meaningful audience participation. The script is on page 146. *Dan Finch*

THE TALK, CHAT, AND RAP SHOW

To pull off this zany series of five skits (pages 151-164), you need a female talk show host that can ad lib as well as follow a script. Ramie's loony cluelessness is the key to the humor in the sketches and to the occasional message in the skits. Ramie's wardrobe suggests she is a New York talk show host—a black hat and a blazer—and she will wear the same basic costume for each skit in the series. *James West*

A REALLY GOOD BOOK

A humorous look at some ways in which the Bible should not be used. Use the script on page 165 to stage this TV talk show spoof. *Mark Vitalis Hoffman*

SEVEN DEADLY SINS
envy
(use selected Proverbs about envy)

CAST	PROPS	
• Andy	• Kitchen table and chairs	• A giant, whole pickle
• Scott	• Plates, etc.	• A magazine
• Nadene	• Cereal boxes	• A door
• Michael	• A take-out deli meal bag and napkins	• An intercom buzzer

The setting: Scott's apartment. ANDY sits at a kitchen table littered with cereal boxes, the remains of a take-out deli meal, and one giant pickle. SCOTT cleans up some plates from dinner.

ANDY: *(looking through magazine)* I gotta lose weight.

SCOTT: Why? You look fine.

ANDY: Fine?…I look fine!?…*(points to magazine model)* This guy looks fine! I look fat.

SCOTT: You don't look fat…you look big…You were made to be big…I was made to be small…Big is good for you.

ANDY: I don't want to be big…you gonna eat that pickle?

SCOTT: No, go ahead. *(intercom buzzes, announcing that someone wants to be let in the security door downstairs)*

ANDY: Did you just call me goat head?

SCOTT: *(answers buzzer)* Yeah?

NADENE: It's me.

SCOTT: C'mon up. *(addresses ANDY)*…It's Nadene…What did you just ask me?

ANDY: Did you call me goat head?

SCOTT: Goat head? No, I said go ahead…have the pickle.

ANDY: Oh. *(examines pickle)* This is a good looking pickle…I wish I looked as good as this pickle… What kind is it?

SCOTT: Vlasic…original whole dill.

ANDY: *(excitedly)* Vlasic! I love Vlasic! They have that Vlasic crunch and crispness. No other pickle has that…It's well chilled.

NADENE: *(enters)* Hey, Scott…hi, Andy…Hey, good-looking pickle. Can I have it?

ANDY: No, you can't have it…Scott said I could have it. He gave it to me and it's my pickle…It's a Vlasic.

NADENE: Ooohh! I love Vlasics…they're so crisp…besides, you need to lose weight! *(grabs the pickle)*

ANDY: There's no weight in a pickle!

NADENE: Andy, think about it. What's on the Vlasic pickle jar…a stork. What do storks bring?… Babies…babies, Andy! Babies, storks, big fat pregnant women, and pickles…it's all connected.

ANDY: So that's why pregnant women are always craving pickles…I never knew.

NADENE: *(sweetly)* Scottie, can I have the pickle?

SCOTT: I really don't care.

ANDY: What! What do you mean you don't care?! You can't give me the pickle and then just decide to give her the pickle…It's already my pickle. I deserve that pickle! Nobody loves Vlasic original whole dills more than I do!

SCOTT: You know…I believe you…Look, what's the big deal? *(grabs the pickle and a knife)* Just cut it in half and then you both can have some of the pickle. *(lifts the knife as if to start cutting)*

ANDY: Nooooo!

NADENE: Waaaiiit!

SCOTT holds the pickle close to him to protect it.

ANDY: Don't kill the pickle, Scott.

SCOTT: Don't kill the pickle? You two are ridiculous…You're acting like this is a family pet that you don't want to be put to sleep…it's a pickle!

NADENE: Do you have any other pickles?

SCOTT: No...it's the last one.

NADENE: Please, Scott...oh, please can I have that pickle?

ANDY: Scott, I want that pickle...I deserve that pickle. *(both scramble towards SCOTT)*

SCOTT: Stop it...stop it. You're both insane. Look, we'll settle this the democratic way.

ANDY: *(looks at NADENE)* ...I'll take evens.

NADENE: I'll take odds.

SCOTT: Best two out of three...for the pickle...no disputes. *(puts pickle in the middle of the table)*

NADENE: *(repeats)* Best two out of three...

ANDY: No disputes.

ANDY and NADENE both put one hand behind their back and make a fist with the other hand in front. On "go" they count to three, shaking their fists with each count. On "shoot" they put out one or two fingers. The total of the fingers determines the winner.

BOTH: One...two...three...shoot! *(ANDY puts out two fingers and so does NADENE)*

ANDY: Even! Yeah!

BOTH: One...two...three...shoot! *(ANDY puts out two and NADENE one)*

NADENE: Odds! All right! *(both take a break to study and stare at each other)*

MICHAEL enters in his best "Kramer" fashion.

SCOTT: Hey, Michael.

MICHAEL looks at ANDY and NADENE curiously.

MICHAEL: Whooaaa!... Nice pickle. *(picks it up)* Vlasic original dill. *(MICHAEL takes a big bite out of the pickle)*

ANDY: Nooooo!

NADENE: Aauuuugghh! *(both jump at MICHAEL, grabbing his throat)*

Characters freeze.

END

SEVEN DEADLY SINS

sloth (or despairing apathy)

1 Kings 19:1-8, Ephesians 5:12-20

CAST	PROPS
• Andy	• Couch
• Scott	• TV
• Nadene	• Junk food containers
• Michael	• Want ads

The scene: ANDY is uninterested in finding a job due to the lack of success he's had up to this point.

The setting: ANDY lays on the couch watching TV, eating cheese balls, drinking a Coke, and basically vegging out. There are a few want ads lying around, but ANDY seems to have given up on them.

NADENE and SCOTT enter together.

NADENE: Hi, Andy. *(ANDY unenthusiastically waves)*

SCOTT: What are you still doing here? I thought you were going for a job interview today?

(ANDY shrugs)

NADENE: Nothing yet, huh? *(ANDY nods, still watching TV)*

SCOTT: *(looking through cereal boxes)* Oh, I can't believe this!

NADENE: *(worried)* What…what is it?

SCOTT: I'm all out of Frosted Flakes!

ANDY: *(without looking up from TV)* Sorry.

SCOTT: *(throws hands up)* Why couldn't you have eaten the Grapenuts?…We got plenty of Grapenuts…you know Frosted Flakes are my favorite. *(MICHAEL enters)*

MICHAEL: *(with empty Frosted Flakes box and bowl)* There you are…you got any Frosted Flakes?

SCOTT: No!…Andy finished off my only box.

MICHAEL: *(reacting)* Aaauuugh!…*(almost crying)* Why didn't you eat the Grapenuts, Andy? I love the Flakes…I love the tiger.

SCOTT: Yeah…well, all I can offer you is Fruity Pebbles. *(tosses MICHAEL the box)*

MICHAEL: *(brightens up)* Oooooh…Yeah! *(catches box of Pebbles)*

SCOTT: So what happened with the interview…did they call?

ANDY: No.

SCOTT: Did they reschedule?

ANDY: Nope.

SCOTT: Well, what happened?

ANDY: I didn't go.

SCOTT: I can see that…How come?

ANDY: I just didn't go.

SCOTT: You just didn't go?…That's not a reason.

ANDY: I didn't feel like it.

SCOTT: You didn't feel like it? You didn't feel like it? Now let me get this straight…you've been looking for a job all summer, and today when you finally have an interview, you don't go because you don't feel like it?

ANDY: *(matter of factly)* Yup.

SCOTT: Andy, you live with your folks…you survive by foraging through my kitchen for cereal…you have no money and you have no life…you need a job.

ANDY: I didn't think I could handle the rejection if they didn't hire me…I've been turned down six times after what I thought were good interviews…I think I'm going to have some kind of emotional breakdown.

SCOTT: Yeah, you look like it.

ANDY: Anyway, I've been looking at a few possibilities I can maybe check out tomorrow. *(motions toward the newspaper)*

NADENE: *(picks up the paper and notices highlighted ad)* Full body massage therapist?

MICHAEL: Ooooh…you ever had one of those, Scott?…They're fantastic!

SCOTT: No…I don't get too excited about the thought of someone like Andy touching parts of my body that I can't even reach.

MICHAEL: Yeeaah!

NADENE: Well, you don't have to have Andy do it…I could call my friend Erica…She gives massages.

SCOTT: Erica…the one that got caught shoplifting?…I don't think so.

ANDY: *(indignantly)* I might make a good massage therapist…Besides, I like working with my hands. *(holds them up to inspect)*

SCOTT: Your hands are covered with powdered cheese…Nobody needs powdered cheese worked into their tired and aching muscles…C'mon, Andy, I hate to sound so parental, but you need to get out there and find a real job.

ANDY: Sorry, Dad…there's nothing out there for me.

MICHAEL: Maybe you'll win the lotto!

SCOTT: Yeah, and maybe he'll land a job as a spokesmodel.

NADENE: It could happen, Scott…my friend Erica knows this guy who…

SCOTT: *(doing his best "Kramer" impression, hold up hand to stop her)* Aaauuuggh!

ANDY: Look, Scott…I appreciate your concern, but right now I'm watching Oprah.

NADENE: Ooooh, Oprah! Who does she have on?

ANDY: Lazy, apathetic men who won't find jobs.

MICHAEL does a double take. ANDY and NADENE look at each other and everybody freezes.

END

SEVEN DEADLY SINS

anger

Matthew 5:21-26, Ephesians 4:25-26

CAST
- Andy
- Scott
- Nadene
- Michael

PROPS
- Table and chairs
- Deck of cards

The scene: SCOTT, MICHAEL, and NADENE are sitting around the table waiting for ANDY so they can play cards together. SCOTT is the most impatient, and when ANDY arrives late, you can tell SCOTT is a little upset.

ANDY enters.

SCOTT: It's about time. Where have you been? We're waiting to play!

NADENE: Hey, Andy. How'd your class go?

MICHAEL: What class?

NADENE: Andy's taking an intro to acting class down at the community center.

MICHAEL: *(dramatically)* The theater!

ANDY: *(excited)* Yeah, it's great! *(surprised)* I'm really liking it.

SCOTT: I didn't know you were taking a class.

ANDY: Well, today was my first day, actually…we worked on mood improvisations.

MICHAEL: *(impressed)* Oooohhh…mood improvisations.

SCOTT: What is that, some kind of theater mumbo jumbo? *(waves arms)*

NADENE: I know…it's a theatrical technique where the actor spontaneously depicts a feeling of emotion suggested by the teacher or director.

ANDY: Yeah!…It was terrific!

MICHAEL: It's kind of like reverse charades.

ANDY: I love charades!

SCOTT: So you're paying tuition to play party games at the community center when you should have been here playing cards with us for free.

ANDY: *(indignantly)* It's not party games…it's acting.

MICHAEL: Well, let's try it.

SCOTT: We're not going to try it…we're going to play cards. We're here to play cards, and cards is what we will play.

NADENE: Why won't you try it, Scott? You scared?

SCOTT: No, I'm not scared.

MICHAEL: You look scared.

SCOTT: I'm not scared.

ANDY: But could you look scared?

SCOTT: Could I look scared?

ANDY: Yeah…let me see you do fear. *(acts theatrical with his hands held up like a producer looking through a camera lens)*

SCOTT gives an impatient look.

NADENE: That's not fear…that's constipation.

SCOTT: *(to ANDY)* Let me see you play cards…can you do that? *(starts dealing cards)*

MICHAEL: *(bragging)* I can do fear.

ANDY: Okay, let's see fear.

MICHAEL prepares himself dramatically and lifts up the cards he's been dealt…reacts with fear.

ANDY: *(matter of factly)* That's not bad.

NADENE: Let me try…Andy, pretend to scare me.

ANDY: Okay…wanna go out on a date with me Friday night?

NADENE: *(shocked and scared, eyes bug out and voice shakes)* Aaauuugh!

SCOTT: Now that's fear…c'mon, let's play cards.

MICHAEL: Give us another one, Andy.

SCOTT: No.

ANDY: All right.

NADENE: Make it harder this time.

SCOTT: No.

ANDY: I wanna see you do a surprise-joy combination.

SCOTT: *(mockingly)* Oooohh…a combination.

NADENE & MICHAEL: *(dramatically respond at the same time and look at SCOTT for a response)* Well?

SCOTT: Well what? *(mockingly mimics them)*

ANDY: That still looks like constipation.

NADENE: Scott, you're not trying.

ANDY: C'mon, Scott, try.

SCOTT: What I'm trying to do is get you guys to play a simple game of cards.

MICHAEL: *(looks at SCOTT)* I've got a good one.

NADENE: What?

MICHAEL: Anger.

SCOTT: *(impatiently)* I'm not doing anger…I'm redealing the cards.

ANDY: That's very subtle…more of a repressed anger. It's reminiscent of a growing impatience with a spice of hidden tension. I think you can project that emotion a little better.

NADENE: C'mon, Scott, let yourself go a bit…think of something that would really drive you mad.

SCOTT: *(slowly)* I'm thinking of something right now…

MICHAEL: Yeeaahh! Express yourself!

SCOTT: *(throws a fit)* I don't want to express myself! *(slams table and MICHAEL falls over)* I want to play cards with my friends…and if that's too much to ask, then maybe they don't really deserve to be my friends at all! Now get out of my apartment before I do something we're all going to regret! *(silence)*

MICHAEL, ANDY, and NADENE get up to leave and talk on their way out.

ANDY: That was really good.

NADENE: Yeah, it was believable… I could feel his rage. It gave me goose bumps.

MICHAEL: Kind of reminded me of DeNiro.

ANDY: You guys wanna go bowling? *(MICHAEL and NADENE respond and nod their heads on the way out)*

SCOTT is left alone on the stage breathing heavily.

END

SEVEN DEADLY SINS
greed

CAST
- Andy
- Scott
- Nadene
- Michael

PROPS
- Table and chairs
- Monopoly game

The scene: Our four characters are playing Monopoly in the kitchen at the table. NADENE is greedy, MICHAEL is carefree, and ANDY is jealous. SCOTT just plays.

ANDY: *(rolls dice)* Nine. *(begins to move piece counting slowly and deliberately; all three begin to count along with him)*…community chest.

NADENE: Why do you have to count out every square?

ANDY: What do you mean?

NADENE: I mean, why do you have to count out EVERY square?

ANDY: I don't want to miss any.

SCOTT: Andy…it's ten squares to a side…every side has ten squares…you're a grown man. You shouldn't have to count every square. You should be able to figure it out just by looking… Do you see Nadene counting every square? No, she can figure it out in her head. *(all this time, MICHAEL is playing with the extra pieces or houses or something)*

ANDY: Yeah, well sometimes I can see her lips moving.

MICHAEL: What's your card say?

ANDY: *(reads card)* Go to jail…go directly to jail! I can't believe this! I've been in jail this whole game! I oughta be able to build houses there.

NADENE: It's where you belong, you felon. Give me the dice, it's my turn.

MICHAEL: You got anything to drink?

SCOTT: *(gets up)* What do you want?

MICHAEL: A root beer float.

SCOTT: A root beer float?

MICHAEL: Yeah. Make it really creamy…and make it foam up when you pour in the root beer.

SCOTT: I don't have any root beer.

MICHAEL: *(disappointed)* Oh…do you have any Snapple?

SCOTT: Yes…what flavor?

MICHAEL: Root beer?

SCOTT: *(getting impatient)* Here's a kiwi-strawberry.

MICHAEL: Ooooh, yeah!

NADENE: Andy, how much will you sell me your railroad for?

SCOTT: Why don't you trade it for a lifetime get-out-of-jail-free card?

ANDY: Very funny…*(looks at NADENE)* For you, I want a thousand dollars and your firstborn male child.

NADENE: For real.

ANDY: I'm serious! You already own half the free world, Leona!

NADENE: *(evilly)* I know…*(rubs her hands together)*

MICHAEL: I'll give you a railroad.

NADENE: *(smiles brightly)* Oooooh…how much?

MICHAEL: *(with a wave of the hand)* No charge.

ANDY: You can't just give her a railroad.

MICHAEL: *(holds property temptingly toward NADENE)* Okay, ten bucks and when we're done you buy me a root beer float.

NADENE: *(grabs property)* Deal! *(puts property with others and wallows in her wealth)*

ANDY: You know she's gonna win! You keep that up and we'll all end up in the poorhouse together, and she'll have everything we own right there in her grubby little hands!

NADENE: *(rolls dice)* Seven. *(picks up her piece and figures in her head while moving lips)* Tennessee…

ANDY: *(to MICHAEL)* That's yours! She owes you rent!

MICHAEL: *(holds up his hand)* No charge.

ANDY: What?!

NADENE: Scott, I want to buy houses before you roll.

SCOTT: Naturally…how many?

NADENE: Here's eight hundred dollars. Give me two houses on Boardwalk and two on Park Place. *(SCOTT takes money and gives the houses)*

MICHAEL: *(still playing with pieces)* Boardwalk is laying out the welcome mat for you, buddy! *(points at SCOTT)*

SCOTT: All right, all right…don't spread your negative vibes by me. I'm in enough trouble as it is.

NADENE: Okay, Scott, you're on Short Line…you need a two to land on Park Place or a four to land on Boardwalk…a six for Mediterranean…eight for Baltic…ten for Reading Railroad…

ANDY: At a hundred bucks a pop!

NADENE: *(smiles)*…and an eleven for Oriental…that's my favorite. *(hands dice to SCOTT)*

SCOTT takes dice with apprehension, and does the sign of the cross with his hand.

ANDY: Just roll.

MICHAEL: Don't mock, Andy, that really works.

SCOTT: *(rolls dice)* Twelve! I got a twelve!… I'm on chance! *(NADENE looks disappointed)* I missed all her properties! *(looks toward heaven)* Thank you…thank you. *(clasps hand in thanks)*

MICHAEL: What's your card say?

SCOTT: Oh yeah. *(looks at card)* Advance…to…Boardwalk. *(NADENE celebrates)* …That's it…I'm out. Here's my money and here's my property.

NADENE: *(rubbing it in)* Just a second, let me make room for storage.

ANDY picks up SCOTT's stuff and slaps it down in front of NADENE, obviously jealous.

NADENE: *(angrily)* I'm taking your stuff next, jail boy! *(ANDY narrows his eyes at NADENE; SCOTT gets up for some cereal; NADENE greedily straightens out property and money while doing inventory)* Let's see…dark purple with hotels…light blues with hotels…reds with hotels…yellows with houses…two utilities…three railroads…and Boardwalk and Park Place with four houses each…and *(counts money)* four thousand dollars…ha, ha, ha.

SCOTT: Take it easy, Nadene, it's just a game.

NADENE: *(snaps back)* It's not just a game, Scott…it's life. This is all a reflection of what life will be like for each of us.

ANDY: This is life?

NADENE: Of course…look at it…Michael has nothing. Scott's out. I have everything, and you're in jail!

SCOTT: She's got a point there… Hey, Michael, wasn't that girl you met at the library going to stop by your place at seven?

MICHAEL: Oooh yeah. Thanks for reminding me.

SCOTT: It's five after seven.

MICHAEL scrambles to leave and in the flustered process knocks the entire game off the table…everyone looks shocked while MICHAEL tries to compose himself as if nothing has happened… Finally, ANDY breaks the silence.

ANDY: Want to go bowling?

SCOTT: Yeah, I think so.

MICHAEL: Sounds like a good idea. *(all three begin to leave the apartment)*

NADENE is left to contemplate her shattered empire.

END

SEVEN DEADLY SINS

gluttony

Proverbs 30:8-9, Isaiah 55:1-5

This sketch takes a different perspective on gluttony.
The sin of gluttony is more than gorging yourself with too much of one thing.
In obsessing with one thing we miss the buffet of gifts the Lord has for us.

CAST
- Andy
- Scott
- Nadene
- Michael

PROPS
- Table and chairs
- Buffet trays
- Dishes with food on them
- Silverware and glasses

The scene: This sketch takes place at a buffet where the three characters enjoy a wide selection of food—except for MICHAEL, who is fixated on stuffing himself with crackers and thereby missing the bounty that's available to him. The scene begins with the four walking from a restaurant buffet to their table, everyone's plates filled with food—except for Michael's plate. He's piled it high with a variety of crackers in those restaurant-size, plastic, individual-serve packages. He eats them one after the other throughout the sketch.

NADENE: This looks delicious.

SCOTT: Yeah, it's really not a bad place…great food…*(looks around)*…casual decor.

ANDY: …and very spacious.

SCOTT: Thanks for treating us, Nadene.

NADENE: No problem.

ANDY: Yeah, thanks.

NADENE: Just call me lucky number seven.

SCOTT: You know, I always wondered if those radio stations actually ever gave away any of the stuff they said they were giving away on the air.

ANDY: What are you saying…you think it's all a scam?

SCOTT: Well, who knows? I mean, maybe they're just saying they're giving away free stuff to get you to listen to their station and maybe they're not giving away free stuff at all. Maybe they have people who pretend to win free stuff working for them in an effort to deceive the rest of us, the unsuspecting public.

ANDY: So maybe there's no free stuff?

SCOTT: Or…maybe there is free stuff, but the radio DJ's are keeping it all for themselves…or giving it away only to their close personal friends… It could be a giant conspiracy…a fraudulent manipulation of the masses.

MICHAEL: Did you ever see *The Sting*?

SCOTT: Ooooh, great movie…thumbs up. *(All four give the thumbs-up signal)*

NADENE: Well, now you know.

SCOTT: Yeah, free buffet dinner for Nadene and her three best friends, compliments of WWWW 99.9…the redundancy station.

ANDY: Playing the same twelve hits over and over and over. *(all three slap high fives and begin to eat, obviously enjoying their food)*…I haven't eaten this good since that deli truck crashed through the front door of our apartment building.

NADENE: This is wonderful. *(with a mouthful of food)*

SCOTT: What do you got there, anyway?

NADENE: Sweet and sour chicken, sweet and sour pork, an egg roll, fried rice, beef teriyaki, bean sprouts, spiced cabbage…and tapioca pudding.

SCOTT: Let me try some of that pudding.

ANDY: I got meat loaf, barbecued chicken, mashed potatoes, corn, cornbread, bread pudding, and about four pounds of strawberry fluff.

NADENE: Oooh, strawberry fluff! *(both SCOTT and NADENE share the fluff)*

MICHAEL: It's toxic.

ANDY: What?… What's toxic?

MICHAEL: *(with crackers in his mouth)* The strawberry fluff…it regenerates spontaneously…my grandma had some in her refrigerator for four months…We kept eating it and eating it and it kept reproducing…it never ran out!

NADENE: Maybe that's why Andy is so big!

SCOTT: *(to MICHAEL)* You've got to be kidding.

MICHAEL: No, I'm serious…it's nuclear!

SCOTT: Well, what are you having then, physics boy?

MICHAEL: Crackers.

NADENE: Crackers? You're just having crackers?

MICHAEL: Yeaaaah!

ANDY: Why are you having just crackers? There's a whole wonderful buffet at your fingertips—and it's free!

MICHAEL: Andy, there's an entire buffet within the cracker kingdom itself!

SCOTT: The cracker kingdom?

MICHAEL: Oh, yeah… I begin with the toastette appetizer, followed by a bunch of robust rye crisps and a few oyster crackers. For the main course I got some saltines, melba toast, and breadsticks with the little sesame seeds on them.

ANDY: *(points to a part of MICHAEL's plate)* What's that one?

MICHAEL: Dessert.

ANDY: Dessert?

MICHAEL: *(holds it up)* Graham crackers.

SCOTT: What are you, a Keebler elf? C'mon, get something from the buffet table.

NADENE: Yeah, Michael, let me get you some nachos.

ANDY: Nachos are crackers, aren't they?

MICHAEL: *(still eating crackers)* Uh-uh…nachos are chips.

NADENE: Do you eat chips?

MICHAEL shakes his head no and gets out spray cheese for his crackers.

SCOTT: Why don't you eat chips?

MICHAEL: Radiation.

SCOTT: Nachos don't have radiation…they have cheese…and tomatoes…and guacamole.

MICHAEL: Same thing.

ANDY: Michael, there's a lot of fantastic food up there, and I can tell you not only is it free from harmful toxins…it's delicious.

NADENE: C'mon , Michael, won't you come get something with me at the buffet?

SCOTT: Yeah, Michael…I saw some homemade, radiation-free, peach cobbler that I know you'll love.

MICHAEL: *(suddenly looking queasy)* I can't.

ALL 3: Why not!?

MICHAEL: …I'm full.

END

SEVEN DEADLY SINS
pride

Proverbs 8:13, 11:2, 13:10, 16:18, 29:23

Pride: thinking of oneself more highly than one ought.

CAST	PROPS
• Andy	• Couch
• Scott	• Magazines, newspapers
• Nadene	• Two pairs of sunglasses
• Michael	

The scene: In SCOTT's apartment. SCOTT and NADENE are sitting silently on a couch reading magazines and newspapers, just minding their own business and relaxing.

MICHAEL enters with his usual spastic flamboyance, dressed in denim jeans and a denim shirt; he sits on the couch between SCOTT and NADENE and slaps an open magazine down on SCOTT's lap and excitedly waits for a response.

SCOTT: *(looking less excited and maybe even a bit annoyed responds innocently)* What?

MICHAEL gestures toward the magazine without saying anything, but strikes a pose as if he's a celebrity eliciting a response.

SCOTT: *(still annoyed and less patient)* What?! What it this? *(mimics the pose)*

MICHAEL: Oh, come on, Scott…look at this right here…what do you see there? *(points to ad in the magazine)*

SCOTT: I don't know…some guy in blue jeans leaning against a bus.

MICHAEL: Nooo…*(holds magazine up to SCOTT's face)*…take a good close look!

SCOTT: *(now annoyed because magazine is in his face)* I can't see anything that close *(pushes magazine back down to his lap and studies the magazine)* …Well, his fly is open.

MICHAEL: *(grabs magazine and holds it up next to his face so SCOTT can see the comparison)* It's me, Scott! I'm the Levi's guy!

SCOTT: *(looks closer)* That's not you.

MICHAEL: *(less excited)* Well…it looks like me.

SCOTT: This guy's black.

MICHAEL: Yeah, but I've been tanning.

NADENE: Let me see.

MICHAEL: Yeah…here. *(shows her the magazine; hopefully)* Now seriously, doesn't that look like me?

NADENE: *(slowly)* Well…you are both wearing denim.

MICHAEL: Exactly… See, Scott, it's me…I'm famous. *(takes out sunglasses and puts them on)*

SCOTT: What are you doing?

MICHAEL: *(in a pompous tone)* Obviously I don't want to be recognized. Scott, once this gets on the street I won't be able to go anywhere…I'll be mobbed, and you know me…I value my privacy.

SCOTT: This from the guy who invites telephone solicitors to call back sometime just to "chat." Look Michael, you're not famous…this isn't you *(pointing to magazine)* and even if it did look like you…which it doesn't…nobody cares.

MICHAEL: *(looking around)* Ssshhhh!…you'll attract a crowd.

ANDY knocks on the door.

MICHAEL: Oh, man, it's starting already!

SCOTT: Come on in.

ANDY: *(enters, walks over, and squeezes onto couch between MICHAEL and NADENE so that all four are sitting together)* What's up?

NADENE: Michael's famous.

ANDY: How come I've never heard of him?

SCOTT: He's not famous. He just thinks he is because he thinks he looks like the model in a Levi's ad. *(hands ANDY the magazine)*

ANDY: *(looks quickly at magazine)* What? I don't see anything.

MICHAEL: Come on…look closer.

ANDY: *(slowly elevates magazine)* Oh my goodness…this is great!…It's unbelievable!

MICHAEL: *(to SCOTT and NADENE)* See I told you so…we could be twins.

ANDY: *(matter of factly)* What, you mean the black guy? No, he looks nothing like you… But this guy! *(points to opposite page)* It's like looking in a mirror! *(slaps magazine down in front of NADENE and strikes his own pose)* What do you think?!

NADENE: You mean the guy in the Pretzels ad?

ANDY: *(expectantly)* Yes!

NADENE: I don't know Andy.

ANDY: Scott?

SCOTT: Uh…no, I don't think so.

MICHAEL: *(leaning over to look)* Oh yeah…that's you buddy…a dead ringer.

ANDY: I'm famous!

SCOTT: I'm nauseated.

ANDY: *(to MICHAEL)* You got any more sunglasses? *(MICHAEL pulls out a spare pair with a big grin on his face. ANDY puts them on proudly while SCOTT and NADENE just shake their heads.)*

MICHAEL: *(to ANDY)* So what are you going to do today?

ANDY: I don't know…maybe watch Oprah.

MICHAEL: Let's go down to the street and stand in front of the building and sign autographs.

SCOTT: I thought you valued your privacy.

ANDY: *(ignoring SCOTT)* You think we can charge for that?

SCOTT: I think you can get arrested for that.

MICHAEL: These people don't understand celebrities…let's get out of here. *(gets up to leave with ANDY)*

SCOTT: *(goes back to his own reading with NADENE)* Well…we'll be looking for you two on "Entertainment Tonight."

MICHAEL: Aaauuugh! *(storms out with ANDY)*

END

SEVEN DEADLY SINS

lust

James 1:13-15

Andy has made a decision to abstain from coffee until marriage (thus the first use of the term "pre-marital cappuccino").
In this sketch coffee is substituted for sexual lust, hopefully allowing the topic to be acted out in a more sensitive way while still getting the idea across to the audience.

CAST	PROPS
• Andy	• Couch, coffee table, chairs
• Scott	• TV
• Nadene	• Three large coffee mugs,
• Michael	filled with coffee

The scene: Our characters are in SCOTT's apartment watching TV and drinking coffee when ANDY enters. SCOTT, NADENE, and MICHAEL are all drinking coffee out of oversized mugs. Throughout the sketch, MICHAEL slurps loudly at his coffee.

ANDY: *(enters apartment and takes off his coat)* The traffic was crazy out there today!

NADENE: Hey Andy, you want to join us?

ANDY: Sure…what you watching?

SCOTT: Some old movie about Elvis in Brazil or something.

NADENE: Yeah, sit down…you want some coffee?

ANDY: No thanks.

SCOTT: You sure…it's one of those special International Flavors flavors.

ANDY: I don't think so.

NADENE: What's the matter? I thought you liked coffee.

ANDY: Well I do…I definitely like coffee.

SCOTT: Then what's the problem? *(MICHAEL slurps)*

ANDY: *(almost embarrassed)* It's just that I've…I've decided to…

SCOTT: Yes?

ANDY: I've decided I'm going to wait until I'm married to have coffee.

NADENE: What?! What do you mean you're waiting until you get married to have coffee?

ANDY: I just see it as an act of intimacy that should really be saved for the context of marriage. It's a special thing between two people. I remember my mom and dad...

NADENE: *(sarcastically)* You can't be serious?

SCOTT: You love coffee! *(MICHAEL slurps)*

ANDY: I know.

NADENE: You have to have coffee. Everybody has coffee!

ANDY: I know everybody has coffee...it's driving me crazy already. It's just that I think it's right to wait. *(getting panicked)* Do you know how hard it is to keep from even thinking about coffee? I'm driving home and everywhere you look...on every corner, in every neighborhood, there's a coffee shop with people wasting their hard-earned money for the quick thrill of satisfying their caffeine craving desire...People waiting for buses with cups of it in their hand. Or I'll be walking the hall at work...

SCOTT: You don't work.

ANDY: Well, figuratively speaking...and I'll catch the smell of Starbucks...

MICHAEL: Oh, they are evil.

ANDY: ...and my upper lip starts sweating. *(MICHAEL slurps)*

SCOTT: How are you going to do this... It's impossible!

ANDY: I know, everywhere I turn I'm assaulted with coffee propaganda...our society is saturated.

MICHAEL: You remember the one guy who got into trouble for having inappropriate coffee with that one woman?

SCOTT: That one guy?...You mean the president? *(MICHAEL just looks at him blankly)* ...with the intern...in the oval office. I think that was something else entirely.

MICHAEL: Yeah, I think you're right...It may have been Ovaltine, after all.

SCOTT: What?

MICHAEL: Ovaltine instead of coffee.

NADENE: Oh, I used to love Ovaltine when I was a little girl…it was so smooth and choco-latey.

MICHAEL: Andy…can you drink Ovaltine?

ANDY: Yes! I can drink Ovaltine. I could drink double espressos and latté grandés if I wanted to…I choose not to. Can't you understand that?

NADENE: *(taking a long, seductive sip of her coffee)* But do you think you can hold out? I mean, what if you never get married. Isn't that going to be hard?

ANDY: Of course it's hard! Especially with people like you around all day!

NADENE: *(still teasing seductively)* C'mon, Andy…have a sip of coffee.

ANDY: Knock it off!

SCOTT: Well, couldn't you get some to go and use some kind of protection?

NADENE: Yeah, like a Styrofoam cup with one of those plastic lids…wouldn't that be okay?

ANDY: No…that's not okay…it's still hot and you can still get burned.

MICHAEL: *(looking at the TV)* Speaking of hot and burned…check out that girl in the pink bikini.

SCOTT: That doesn't leave much to the imagination.

NADENE: Do people actually find that attractive?

ANDY: Oh my goodness…she's drinking a cup of coffee.

SCOTT: On such a hot day? Why not Lemonade or diet Coke?

NADENE: Hey Andy…your upper lip is starting to sweat. *(MICHAEL slurps)*

ANDY: I gotta get out of here. *(wipes upper lip, grabs coat, and leaves)*

NADENE: Good luck.

SCOTT: *(shouts after ANDY)* If you run into Juan Valdez tell him we said hi.

NADENE: Cheers. *(all three clang their cups and slurp loudly)*

END

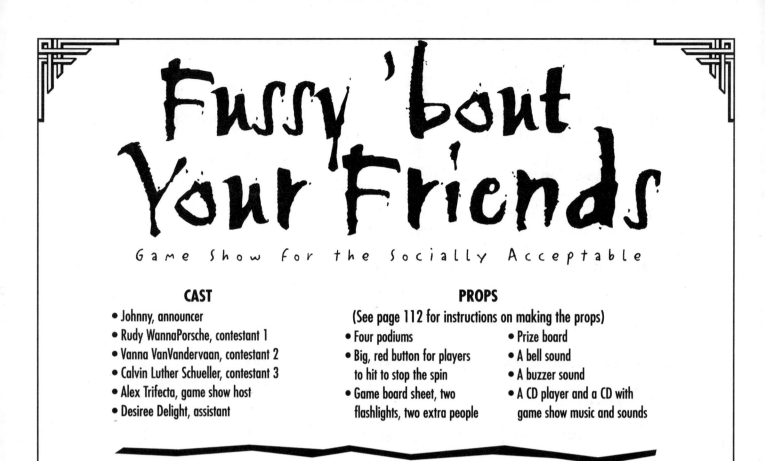

Fussy 'bout Your Friends

Game Show for the Socially Acceptable

CAST
- Johnny, announcer
- Rudy WannaPorsche, contestant 1
- Vanna VanVandervaan, contestant 2
- Calvin Luther Schueller, contestant 3
- Alex Trifecta, game show host
- Desiree Delight, assistant

PROPS
(See page 112 for instructions on making the props)
- Four podiums
- Big, red button for players to hit to stop the spin
- Game board sheet, two flashlights, two extra people
- Prize board
- A bell sound
- A buzzer sound
- A CD player and a CD with game show music and sounds

Arrange props to stage a game show. Play introductory music as ANNOUNCER speaks.

ANNOUNCER: *(from an off-stage microphone)* Ladies and gentlemen, welcome to the show where image is king, Lady Luck is queen, and a little knowledge is a dangerous thing. And now, here's your host, Alex Trifecta!

Alex enters expecting applause. If he doesn't get it, he exits and enters again to a more enthusiastic introduction.

Ladies and gentlemen, I present to you the game show host of game show hosts, a man among men, a legend in his own mind. The one, the only, Alex Trifecta!!!

Alex re-enters, hopefully to thunderous applause.

ALEX: Thank you, Johnny, and thank you in our studio audience. Welcome to "Fussy 'Bout Your Friends." As you know, we play the game with three contestants, all competing for image, position, happiness, and success in life through the accumulation of desirable friendships. Johnny, let's meet our challengers.

As each name is called, that CONTESTANT enters, shakes hands with ALEX, and goes to his or her podium.

ANNOUNCER: Okay, Alex. First, a real estate investor from Make-a-Buck Valley in Southern California—meet Rudy WannaPorsche.

138

ALEX: Interesting name, Rudy. WannaPorsche—is that Native American?

RUDY: No, Alex. I'm actually Italian, German, French, Austrian, Japanese, and Swedish.

ALEX: Nice to have you on the show, Rudy.

ANNOUNCER: Next, a philosophy professor from Superior State in upstate New York—meet Vanna VanVandervaan.

ALEX: Interesting name, Vanna. VanVandervaan—is that Dutch?

VANNA: No, Alex. It's actually Native American.

ALEX: Well, good luck today, Vanna. Johnny?

ANNOUNCER: Last, we welcome Calvin Luther Schuller, a seminary student from Orthodox University.

ALEX: Interesting name, Calvin…

CALVIN: *(interrupting)* I'm Dutch.

ALEX: Well, let's get started, shall we? You know the rules. We'll be competing for fantastic take-home prizes in the form of fabulous friendships. Each contestant is allowed up to four spins on the big FBYF board. With each spin you can gain desirable friendships and associations that will bring you a happy, fulfilling, and rewarding life. After each spin a player may choose to stop and keep the friendship prizes he or she has accumulated on the prize board, or risk it all and continue to spin. If at any time a player lands on a relationship Whammy, that player forfeits all prizes and is obliged to carry out the Whammy command in their own hometown.

Rudy, you won the toss backstage and will spin first. *(RUDY raises his fists overhead with a big smile and moves to the red button)* Let's start the board, and Rudy, you hit the magic stop button when you're ready.

The board noise begins and lights randomly travel across the board. When Rudy hits the red button, a bell rings and the lights land on the Wealth & Fame square.

Congratulations, Rudy. You've landed on our Wealth & Fame square. *(Rudy celebrates)* Let's put that prize up on your side of the board. Your friends will be well known and well off. You've got to feel good about that.

RUDY: Thank you, Alex. I do.

ALEX: Do you want to keep the Wealth & Fame friendships and go home? Or do you want to risk it and spin again!

If the audience doesn't start urging him to spin, ALEX can ask them, "What do you think, studio audience?" to encourage participation.

RUDY: I'll spin again, Alex. *(audience cheers)*

ALEX: Okay, let's start the board up for Rudy. *(lights and board noise)* Stop it when you're ready.

RUDY: C'mon, no Whammies. Big friendships. *(hits red button)* Stop! *(lights stop on lampshade; bell sounds; Rudy reacts excitedly)*

ALEX: That's the lampshade square. Rudy, you've just won friends that will always be fun and happy. The life-of-the-party kind of people.

RUDY: Awesome! I've always wanted friends like that…and I'll bet they've got money, too!

ALEX: Well, Rudy, we'll put that one up on your side of the prize board. Do you want to stop, or risk it all and go on?

RUDY: *(plays to the crowd)* I'll spin!

ALEX: Okay, here we go! Start the board. *(lights and board noise)*

RUDY: No Whammies, no Whammies! *(hits red button)* Stop! *(lights stop on GQ; bell sounds; happily)* All right!

ALEX: That's our GQ square, Rudy. You've won friends who are beautiful people. Put that up on the board. Imagine that, Rudy—wealth, fame, fun, and beauty. Looks like life could be one big party. Will you stop or risk it all on one more spin for the big bonus bonanza prize here on "Fussy 'Bout Your Friends"?

RUDY: *(thinks it over)* I'll spin!

ALEX: Okay, here we go, Rudy. It's your last spin. Start the board. *(lights and board noise)*

RUDY: No Whammies. Big friendships! *(hits red button)* Stop! *(lights stop on Whammy; buzzer sounds)*

ALEX: Oh, too bad, Rudy. You've been Whammied. Of course, that means you lose your prizes on the big board. Johnny, tell Rudy about what he'll go home with.

ANNOUNCER: Rudy, you've landed on our Mother Teresa Whammy. According to the command of Christ, you will have the opportunity to go home and befriend the orphans and widows, the poor and homeless, the hungry, sick, and the dying. Too bad, Rudy.

  140

ALEX: Well, Rudy, you had a nice run going there. I'm sorry.

RUDY: *(hangs his head)* Yeah, yeah, yeah. *(returns dejectedly to his podium)*

ALEX: Vanna, you're up next. Are you ready to play our game?

VANNA: Absolutely, Alex. *(steps briskly forward to shake hands with ALEX and take her place at the red button)*

ALEX: Good luck, and let's start the board for Vanna. *(lights and board noise)*

VANNA: *(composed, dignified, and quick to hit the red button)* Stop! *(lights stop at DDBAPDQ; bell sounds)*

ALEX: Hey, it's our DDBAPDQ square. Vanna, you've won friends that are educated and degreed. Let's put that up on the board. Now will you…

VANNA: *(interrupting)* I'll spin.

ALEX: Okay, here we go. *(lights and board noise)*

VANNA: *(hits red button)* Stop! *(lights stop at Big Brain; bell sounds)*

ALEX: All right, Vanna. You've landed on our Big Brain square, which of course means we will add to your side of the prize board friends who are bright and stimulating. Very important, I'm sure, to someone in your academic field. Now, what do you want to do?

VANNA: I'll spin. Start the board.

ALEX: You heard her, boys. Start the board. *(lights and board noise)*

VANNA: *(hits red button)* Stop! *(lights stops at gavel and ladder; bell sounds)*

ALEX: That's the gavel and ladder square. Vanna, we'll add to your prize total friends that are in high positions of power and prestige. Again, an excellent prize. Do you…

VANNA: *(interrupting)* I'll spin.

ALEX: Here we go again for a clean sweep and a shot at the big bonus bonanza prize.

VANNA: C'mon, no Whammies! *(hits red button)* Stop! *(lights stop at Whammy; buzzer sounds)* Noooooooo!

ALEX: Oh, sorry, Vanna. You lose your prizes. Johnny, tell her what she gets to take home instead.

ANNOUNCER: Vanna, you've landed on our Least of These Whammy. According to the heart of Christ, you will welcome little children. You will befriend the elderly and give an ear to those who are emotionally hurting. You will also have to be friends with _____!

(someone in your audience)

VANNA: Not _____!

(same someone)

ALEX: Don't worry, Vanna. You'll get used to it. *(VANNA whirls sharply away and returns to her podium)* Calvin, I guess that leaves you.

CALVIN: *(steps out to meet ALEX and shakes hands)* I'm ready to play, Alex! *(moves to the red button)*

ALEX: Well, then, let's start the board and see what happens. Good luck! *(lights and board noise)*

CALVIN: *(eyes raised to heaven and hands folded in prayer)* I don't need luck. *(hits red button)* Stop! *(lights stop at R&R; bell sounds)* Hallelujah!

ALEX: That's right, Calvin. You've hit our R&R square. So we'll put up on your side of the board friends who are respectable and religious. I'm sure that will be quite an asset. Now, will you play or quit?

CALVIN: I'll play on!

ALEX: Let's start the board, and good luck.

CALVIN: C'mon, no Whammies. Big friendships. Hail, Mary. *(hits red button; lights stop at No Dice; bell sounds)* Praise the Lord!

ALEX: Congratulations, Calvin. That's our No Dice Square. We're going to put up on your side of the board friends who are morally superior. They don't gamble, they don't cheat, drink or fool around. Again, a nice addition for you. Play on, Calvin? Or stop?

CALVIN: I'll play on.

ALEX: Stop the board when you're ready, Calvin.

CALVIN: C'mon, no Whammies. No Whammies. *(hits red button)* Stop! *(lights stop at Ivory soap; bell sounds)* Excellent!…uh, I mean, glory!

ALEX: Let's see. You've landed on our Ivory Soap square, which of course means we'll add to your prize total friends who are clean and conservative—just like yourself. Well, Calvin, that's an impressive prize package of friendships. Will you take what you have and go home, or risk it all with one more spin for the big Fussy 'bout Your Friends bonanza prize?

142

CALVIN: I'll…I'll…I'll spin!

ALEX: Okay, Calvin. Good luck. Jump in when you're ready.

CALVIN: C'mon, no Whammies. Big friendships. Please, please, please… *(hits red button)* Stop! *(lights stop on Whammy; buzzer sounds; CALVIN's mouth drops open in disbelief)*

ALEX: Oh Calvin, you've Whammied out. Let's take your prizes off the board and have Johnny tell you what you'll be taking home instead.

ANNOUNCER: Calvin, you've landed on the Mind of Christ Whammy. In obedience to the example of Christ, you will go home and associate with people of the streets. In the words of Jesus' day, you will "eat with prostitutes, tax collectors, and sinners." *(CALVIN buries his face in his hands and stumbles back to his podium)*

ALEX: Good luck explaining that one to the wife and kids. We have consolation prizes for each of you off stage. Thank you for playing and thank you for watching. Until next time, this is Alex Trifecta saying, When you're fussy 'bout your friends, you may be in for a big surprise.

ANNOUNCER: "Fussy 'bout Your Friends" is brought to you by Good News Productions in association with James Chapter 2 Studios. Special thanks to God above, who does not show favoritism, and to our creative consultant, Jesus of Nazareth, known locally as a friend of sinners.

Play departure music while Alex and guests shake hands and leave the stage.

END

The Player

CAST

- Carolyn Leftowich, host
- Craig Vaughn, player

CAROLYN: Good evening, ladies and gentlemen. Welcome to "Look Who's Talking." I'm your host, Carolyn Leftowich. Please join me in welcoming our special guest, Mr. Craig Vaughn.

CRAIG: *(enters wearing a baseball uniform)* Thank you, thank you.

CAROLYN: Thanks for joining us today, Craig. That certainly is a nice uniform you're wearing.

CRAIG: Thank you, Carolyn. It's the team uniform.

CAROLYN: Did you grow up dreaming of becoming a baseball player?

CRAIG: I always knew one day I'd be wearing this uniform.

CAROLYN: How exciting. I guess you have to work out every day to be in shape for the team.

CRAIG: Actually, I don't work out.

CAROLYN: I guess you get enough exercise just practicing with the team.

CRAIG: I don't practice, either.

CAROLYN: Wow! You must be pretty good not to have to practice. I suppose you study the Play Book a lot, then?

CRAIG: I skimmed through the pages once, but I don't really study it. I don't have the time.

CAROLYN: You mean, you're on the team but you don't work out, you never practice, and you don't have time to read the Play Book?

CRAIG: That's right. But I'm at every game—that is, unless I have I have something better to do.

CAROLYN: What does your coach say about that?

CRAIG: I don't know. We never talk to each other.

CAROLYN: You never talk to the coach?

CRAIG: You know how it is—he's busy with other people, I'm busy with my life…you know!

CAROLYN: Let me get this straight. You're a team player, but you don't work out, you don't practice with the team, you don't have time to read the Play Book, you miss games when you have something better to do, and you never talk to the coach.

CRAIG: That's right.

CAROLYN: What position do you play?

CRAIG: Pitcher.

CAROLYN: Pitcher? But the pitcher's like the heart of the team. How do you play that position without ever practicing, studying, or talking to the coach?

CRAIG: Play? Oh, I don't play. I might get hurt.

CAROLYN: You don't play?

CRAIG: No, I just sit on the bench and watch.

CAROLYN: You sit on the bench and watch. Wouldn't it be more accurate to say that you merely call yourself a player, but that in reality, you just sit there in your fancy uniform, watching the real players?

CRAIG: That's putting it rather harshly.

CAROLYN: Well, there you have it, folks…until next week…I'm Carolyn Leftowich coming to you live on "Look Who's Talking."

END

Tool Time
RESTORATION GOSPEL

CAST
- Heidi
- Tim Taylor
- Al Borland
- Jill Taylor
- Wilson

PROPS
- A wood frame chair with a fabric seat — in need of refinishing
- Two large boxes or barriers
- A floppy garden hat for Wilson

HEIDI: Hi, my name is Heidi. Tonight we have a special treat for _____! Right here in the sanctuary we are going to tape a
(the name of your church)
segment of one of your favorite shows, "Tool Time." As you know, the audience is an important part of the show. So when I say, "Does everybody know what time it is?" what do you say?

Prompt the AUDIENCE to shout, "It's tool time."

HEIDI: Right. But when Tim "the Toolman" Taylor comes on stage, you need to yell it even louder. Let the neighborhood know that _____.
(the name of your church)
audiences get excited. Let's practice once more: Does everybody know what time it is?

AUDIENCE: It's tool time!

HEIDI: That was great. Now this time is for real. Five, four, three, two, one: Does everybody know what time it is?

AUDIENCE: It's tool time!

HEIDI: And here's your "Tool Time" host, Tiiiim Taylor.

Applause.

TIM: Thank you, Heidi. Thank you everyone. I'm Tim Taylor, and you all know my assistant, Al Borland.

AL does two-finger salute. Applause.

TIM: Today on "Tool Time" we are going to talk about restoration. You can build with the finest wood and craftsmanship, but over the years things can happen.

AL: Especially around you, Tim.

TIM: *ANYBODY* might innocently set a hot soldering iron down on his wife's great grandmother's chair, or use it to reach the top shelf in the linen closet and forget to take his golf cleats off.

AL: Anybody, Tim?

TIM: Or Al's mother might sit on it, but that show wouldn't be about restoration—it would be about reconstruction. Anyway, this is my wife's chair and we have the stripping solution ready to take off all the old varnish and paint. *(holds up large chair and carries it to box or barrier)*

AL: Uh, Tim, have you checked the concentration of that solution?

TIM: It's all right, Al. *(puts big chair into box or behind barrier)*

AL: Uh, Tim…

TIM: Not now, Al. We just put the chair in the solution and do our little stripping dance. *(TIM hams up a spontaneously choreographed dance)*

AL: Uh, Tim…

TIM: *(dancing around)* La cu-ca-racha, old chair I gotcha.

147

AL: Uh, Tim…

TIM: *(shaking box)* This is the way we clean the chair from all its deep and dark despair.

AL: Uh, Tim…

TIM: What is it, Al?

AL: Tim, are you sure you are supposed to leave the chair in that long?

TIM: *(looks at his watch)* Sure, Al. I think it's probably ready right about now. *(smiling as he pulls out the chair—like a rabbit out of a hat—he is shocked to see the chair has shrunk.)*

AL exits and TIM walks over to a second barrier behind which WILSON is concealed.

HEIDI: And now a word about Binford Tools. We've all heard the adage, "If you want the job done right, do it yourself." But the new Binford Tool line changes all that. Now we can practically guarantee that no matter who does the job—and in present company *(indicating TIM with a jerk of her head)* we don't say this lightly—"If you want the job done right, do it with Binford tools."

TIM leans toward the barrier. All the audience can see of WILSON is his floppy, brimmed hat.

WILSON: Hi-de-ho, neighbor.

TIM: Hi, Wilson.

WILSON: You look troubled, Tim. Another explosion on the show?

TIM: No, no, no, it's nothing like that. We restored one of Jill's old chairs, and it got me to wondering—what does a person do when they need to be restored? Is there some kind of pain stripper you dip a person in that leaves a him ready to be made like new?

WILSON: It's a tough job to refurbish the smudges and tarnish that mar people on the inside.

TIM: And you can't do a ring and valve job on yourself, either.

WILSON: That's true. It's like my cousin Billy Graham said at our family reunion when he quoted Romans 3:23, "For all have sinned and fall short of the glory of God." But there is a kind of dipping that does take make a person new, Tim.

TIM: Uuuuh?

WILSON: I believe it was the writer of Hebrews who said, "How much more will the blood of Christ...cleanse our consciences from acts that lead to death." And the Apostle Paul wrote in 2 Corinthians 5:17, "Therefore, if anyone is in Christ, he is a new creation; old things have passed away; behold all things have become new.

TIM: *(shaking his head thoughtfully)* Thanks, Wilson. *(JILL enters; TIM leaves Wilson to go to JILL)*

TIM: Jill, I was just talking to Wilson about getting rid of my defects.

JILL: That must have been a long conversation.

TIM: It's like the inventor of graham crackers said when he went to Hebrew school, next to God we're all short, and fall down because we trip over our sin...But if we have faith we're like the hot rod.

JILL: What are you talking about, Tim?

TIM: Well, it's like if we go to God's car wash, he bores out our engines and beefs up our suspension. Then God gives us about 20 coats of lacquer and hand rubs us out, so when we are in God's light and people look at us, we shine.

JILL: No, Tim, you don't quite understand.

TIM: *(getting defensive)* Of course I do.

JILL: Everyone is sinful, and this separates them from God.

TIM: That's not good, is it?

JILL: No, because the penalty for sin is death.

TIM: Uuuh? Don't worry about me, Jill; I've decided not to sin any more.

JILL: Really?

TIM: Sure, you women have a hard time with this sin stuff, but we MEN…we just make up our minds and it's as good as done.

JILL: But Tim, the penalty for sin is eternal death.

TIM: Uuuuunh?

JILL: Yes, and all your past sins count, too.

TIM: Uuunnh? *(thinking)* Well, what's the answer?

JILL: The answer is Jesus. He paid the penalty for you by dying on the cross.

TIM: *(with bravado)* So…I'm okay…got it covered…no problemo.

JILL: You're not covered unless you accept Jesus as your Savior and Lord. Salvation is a gift God offers you, but you have to reach out and take it.

TIM: What happens if I take God's gift?

JILL: Then, like Wilson said, God begins to restore you. He changes your life—helps you to do his will and resist temptation. He sends the Holy Spirit to give you more power to live obedient to God.

TIM: MORE POWER!! Uuunh unnnh. That's for me. Can I accept this gift right now?

Both kneel facing each other.

HEIDI: It's a take.

END

The TALK, CHAT, & RAP SHOW Series

THE JONESES

CAST
- Ramie, abrasive and clueless talk show host
- Mr. and Mrs. Jones, average, middle-income couple

PROPS
- Couch and chair or three chairs

Ramie is dressed to parody a New York talk show host. Oblivious to the condition of her guest or to what her guest specializes in, fumbles words, talks too fast, and often has to ask for audience assistance.

RAMIE: *(stands in front of her chair)* Good evening, every buddy, and welcome to the Chat, Shalk, and Chap Show. I mean the Chalk, Tap, and Rat Show, well you know what I mean. Today we have with us…Who is our guest…Oh, that's right…I have on the show today the couple we all know as Mr. and Mrs. Jones. Let's all welcome them. *(applause)*

Mr. and Mrs. Jones enter and stand awkwardly on stage because RAMIE has neglected to invite them to sit down.

MR. JONES: Thank you.

MRS. JONES: Yes, thank you. Wow, you have quite a crowd tonight.

RAMIE sits down. MRS. JONES looks at the other chairs and edges back to sit in one of them. As MR. JONES speaks she pulls at his hand until he also sits down.

MR. JONES: Yes, I just want you to know we watch your show every time it's on.

MRS. JONES: What's the name of it again?

RAMIE: It's the Ralk, Chap, and Tat Show, I mean the…never mind. Anyway, our topic is "measuring up." Tell us what you know about this topic.

MR. JONES: Well, as everyone knows, the Lord has blessed us with a lot of nice things.

RAMIE: *(catty)* Oh, really? How do we know that?

MR. JONES: Well, we <u>are</u> the Joneses.

RAMIE: *(doesn't get the allusion)* Oh, right!?

MRS. JONES: With my husband's good job, we can afford to have just about anything we want.

RAMIE: Wow, that's pretty neat.

MR. JONES: We have the nicest house in the neighborhood, the best appliances, tools, furniture, cars, gifts, etc.…

MRS. JONES: That's right.

Pause.

RAMIE: *(reacts like they haven't hit the topic)* Right, go on…

MR. JONES: Well, that's it.

RAMIE: So what does that have to do with the topic?

MR. JONES: You don't get it, do you?

RAMIE: *(sarcastically)* You don't get it, do you? That's it! Where's my guest coordinator? These guys are clueless. They're half a brick short of a full deck.

MR. & MRS. JONES look at each other and try to figure out what she just said.

MRS. JONES: Wait, Wait. I'll explain a little further.

RAMIE: *(sarcastically)* Well, how thoughtful.

MRS. JONES: Every time we get some new furniture or a new car, the Smiths next door always try to upstage us in some way, but they don't really have the means to do it.

RAMIE: So, how do they keep up?

MR. JONES: They get themselves more and more in debt just to keep up with us.

RAMIE: Well, why do they feel that they have to have everything you have?

MRS. JONES: I don't know. I mean, we don't have to have all these nice things to be happy.

RAMIE: Oh, yeah, prove it. How about giving everything to me, and we'll see if you're still happy.

MR. JONES: No, I'm afraid that's not the point.

RAMIE: Okay, well then, would somebody please tell me the point! Why does everybody have to keep up with the *(points to MR. & MRS. JONES)* Joneses! *(looks at watch)* Okay, well, we are out of time…*(startled by a sudden insight)* Oh, I get it…So you're the Joneses Joneses…Keeping up with the Joneses! Well, thank you Mr. and Mrs. Jones for being on our show today.

And thank you, studio audience, for joining me on the Tap, Cat, and Shat Show.

Lights fade.

END

The TALK, CHAT, & RAP SHOW Series

KLEPTOMANIAC

CAST
- Ramie, abrasive and clueless talk show host
- Susie Sticky Fingers, kleptomaniac

PROPS
- Bald cap for Ramie
- Foundation makeup
- Black wig
- Couch and chairs
- Department store shopping bag
- Things for Susie to steal: bracelet, ashtray, watch, jewelry, a CD, flower in a vase, money, pen, hair clamp, etc.

Set: Couch and chair or three chairs.

RAMIE wears a bald cap for this skit. Over the bald cap she wears a wig and also her regular black hat. Use foundational make-up on Ramie's bald cap as well as on her face so she looks as if she's bald. When Susie steals things during the show, Ramie is looking away and doesn't see it happen.

SUSIE STICKY FINGERS holds a department store shopping bag into which she puts the things she steals.

RAMIE: Good evening everybody, and welcome to the Chip, Chapped, and Chalk Choe…welcome to the Talk, Tat, and Tap Toe…the Ralk, Rat, and Rap Show. This week we're going to answer the question, what is a kle… ptoe… mmmahh… nihac… clepto… mah… han… ti… hac… Could somebody help me?

Somebody from the audience yells, "Kleptomaniac."

RAMIE: Thank you! It just so happens that we have a klepto…mani…uh, whatever with us on the show today. Would you please welcome Ms. Sticky Susie Fingers. *(stands to welcome guest)* It's such a pleasure for you to be on my show, I mean for me to have you on my show tonight, how are you?

SUSIE: I'm doing just fine.

RAMIE: That's good. So tell me about this kleptomania thing. What effects does it have on you? *(looks into the audience, smiling and making eye contact)*

SUSIE: *(steals bracelet)* It has certain benefits. *(twirls bracelet)*

RAMIE: *(looks down at a loose thread in the couch)* What kind of benefits?

SUSIE: *(steals an ash tray)* Well, being a kleptomaniac allows you to acquire a lot of nice things.

RAMIE: What kind of nice things?

SUSIE: *(steals a watch)* Watches, bracelets, Gucci purses, etc.

RAMIE: Wow! I wish I was a klepto! I could sure use a Gucci purse, or even just a Liz Claiborne purse. How do you acquire such nice things?

SUSIE: *(steals large hair clamp; whispers)* I steal them.

RAMIE: I'm sorry, can you turn *(bangs on microphone)* up the microphone, I couldn't hear what she said. Okay, say again.

SUSIE: I said…I steal them.

RAMIE: *(nonchalant)* Oh, okay. So…*(excited)* YOU DO WHAT?! YOU STEAL THEM! What if you get caught? Why do you…do that?

SUSIE: Well, I don't mean to, *(steals photograph)* I mean, I don't do it on purpose.

RAMIE: *(nonchalant)* Oh, well, that's good… *(get excited)* RIGHT, I'M SO SURE, for some reason I don't BUY that!

SUSIE: *(steals money)* BUY? What's that mean?

RAMIE: You know, when you go to the store and pay money for things.

SUSIE: Oh, is that what this green stuff is for? *(shows money)*

RAMIE: Yes, that's right! Say, that's a lot of money.

SUSIE: *(steals a pen)* I have a lot of it, but I don't know what to do with it.

RAMIE: *(reaches out and snatches the money)* Give it to me, I'll show you what to do with it. Now, let's get back to the issue. You mean that you steal but you don't mean to?

SUSIE: Yep, that's what the doctor said.

RAMIE: Wait, you're not going to steal anything from me are you? I won't put up with that on the Talk, Hat, and Hap show. No ma'am. Not on my show.

SUSIE: May God strike me dead if I even think about it. *(steals flower from the vase; lightning sound effects, lights up and down. SUSIE hugs RAMIE when the lights go down and steals a necklace)*

RAMIE: Girl, get off me. I don't want to get struck. There's something weird about you, honey. You better not steal anything on the Salk, Sat, and Sap So…

SUSIE: Oh, no, I would never try to steal the show. *(takes microphone)* Besides, a distinguishing factor of kleptomaniacs is that they never steal from talk show hosts.

RAMIE: *(grabs the microphone back)* That's a good rule, honey. Make sure you always remember me as a talk show host. Well, we would like to thank Stusie Sicky Fingers for coming on the show and sharing with us tonight.

SUSIE steals RAMIE's wig, exposing the host's bald head, and exits, lugging her bag of things

RAMIE: *(not noticing her wig is gone)* Next time we meet, we'll be investigating the phenomenon of scissorfrania, er pizzamania,

Someone from the audience yells, "schizophrenia."

Thank you, and thank you, studio audience, for joining us on the Balk, Chat, and Bap show.

Lights down.

END

The TALK, CHAT, & RAP SHOW Series

OXYMORONS

CAST
- Ramie, abrasive and clueless talk show host
- Guest, male; nicely dressed, professional

PROPS
- Desk and chairs

Set: Desk and chair. RAMIE needs to be blond for this sketch.

RAMIE: Hello everybody, and welcome to the Talk and the Rap and the Ch…I mean the Chalk, Tat, and the Rap…The Talk, Chat, and Rap Show. Today our guest is an oxymarone, no an oximorane, oxi…would somebody please help me?

Somebody in the audience yells, "Oxymoron!"

RAMIE: Yes, oxymaroni, thank you. Let's please welcome our oxtimoron. *(stands to greet guest)*

GUEST: *(enters)* It's great to be on your show today. What's the name of it again?

RAMIE: It's the Talk and the Rap and the Shat Choe. I mean it's the…

GUEST: *(interrupts)* Never mind, I get the picture.

Both sit down.

RAMIE: Okay, well it's so neat having an oxymorone on the show today. I've never had one on the show before.

GUEST: I'm not an…

RAMIE: *(interrupts)* So tell me what are you. I mean what is an oxtymacaroni?

GUEST: Well first, I'm not an…

RAMIE: *(interrupts)* Wait! Let me guess. It's a moron with a pimple problem!

GUEST: No, please, you don't understand. I'm not an…

RAMIE: No, no I got it it's a…

GUEST: *(yell)* Would you shut up and let me talk?!

RAMIE: Wait a minute this is MYYY SHOW! You're making me very mad! I'm in control here. This is my floor and you cannot have it unless I give it to you. Okay, you can have the floor now, because I gave it to you!

GUEST: *(sarcastically)* Well, thank you ever so kindly. First, I am not an oxymoron.

RAMIE: What are you doing on my show then? The topic today is oxymacaroons. Where's the guest coordinator?

GUEST: No, wait. Would you just let me spit it out?

RAMIE: Okay…NO! You better not spit on my show. No sir…

GUEST: An oxymoron is a literary term that uses two words that normally contradict each other, but together have a profound meaning…

RAMIE: Oh…can you give me an example?

GUEST: I'd be glad to. "Deafening silence."

RAMIE: That's me after my parents yell at me. I usually can't hear anything for a couple of hours.

GUEST: "Safe sex."

RAMIE: *(reaches over and covers her mouth)* Don't say that WORD…Not in front of my people. My daddy always said, "Save *(say sex without the "x")* seeeeee" for marriage.

GUEST: That's right. Here's another one—"military intelligence."

RAMIE: That's really funny…I like that…wait a minute my dad is in the military. You take that back!

GUEST: Do what? Here's another one—"Stable Female."

RAMIE: *(starts to laugh and then catches herself)* Oh that's…WHAT! That's a rather chauvinistic remark…

GUEST: If the shoe fits…

RAMIE: Oh, so I suppose now this is a show on clichés.

GUEST: Oh wait, here's another one: "Smart Blonde."

RAMIE: *(laughs hysterically and then stops and grabs her hair and looks at it)* Hey!! *(pause)* Wait. I've got one. How about "Beverly Hillbillies." You know a bunch of rednecks living in Beverly Hills. That's kinda contradisory, contradistory, controdiceory…

Someone in the audience yells, "contradictory!"

RAMIE: That's it.

GUEST: Here's another one…

RAMIE: Hey, wait. Try "Sensitive Male" on for size.

GUEST: You just insulted me! That's it; I'm leaving. This show is a disgrace to journalism.

GUEST exits

RAMIE: Wait, here's a cliché for you. If it's too hot in the kitchen…something or other. I think I struck a nerve. *(laugh)* Anyway this has been another edition of the Talk, Chat, and Rap Show. Oh wait, I just thought of another one…"honest politician."

Pause for audience's response.

RAMIE: Well, that wraps up the show. We'll see you next time.

Lights down.

END

Set: Desk with two chairs.

The TALK, CHAT, & RAP SHOW Series

PYROMANIACS

CAST
- Ramie, abrasive and clueless talk show host
- Mr. Pyro, male; pale face (use white foundation make-up)

PROPS
- Either a video screen with a viceo clip of fire and/or sound effects of a fire
- Matches and two lighters
- Two beakers: one with water and one with alcohol
- Cloth and tongs to hold burning cloth away from you
- Tray to carry beakers on
- A bucket of water

At the point in the show where the lights go down, PYRO dips a damp cloth that has been wrung out in the rubbing alcohol. He holds one end of the cloth with the tongs and lights the bottom end of the cloth. As soon as the flame takes, play the video of fire or the fire sound effects.

RAMIE will take out a powder puff of soot and blacken her face to make it look smoke damaged. She'll mess up her hair and stumble her way in front of the desk.

NOTE: To put the fire out, dip the burning rag in the bucket of water. Be sure to rehearse this before trying it on stage.

RAMIE: Welcome to the Talk, Shrat, and the Tap Toe. Okay. First of all today we have on the show a pie-rye-maniac. A py-ro-miniac.

Someone from the audience says, "Pyromaniac."

RAMIE: That's right and thank you very much. His name is Mr. Pyro. So please welcome Mr. Pyro. (clap hands and stand)

MR. PYRO enters carrying a tray of beakers, tongs, matches, lighters, and bucket of water. RAMIE extends her hand to shake his hand. MR. PYRO just looks at her hand. RAMIE takes deep breath and nonchalantly fixes hair with the hand she extended. MR. PYRO sits down. As he sits he constantly lights matches and throws them in a bucket of water.

RAMIE: (sits down) Can you tell me, what exactly is a pyromaniac?

MR. PYRO is still lighting matches and intently watching the flame.

RAMIE: (gently puts her hand on his) Don't do that!

MR. PYRO moves hand and keeps lighting the matches.

RAMIE: *(takes matches)* Oh my gosh. We need to get him off…

MR. PYRO: *(yells)* Shut up! *(pulls out lighter and keeps lighting lighter)*

RAMIE: *(jumps a little)* Sorry. Uh, Mr. Pyro… *(grabs lighter; uses positive voice)* You gotta give me that because you can't do that on the show. *(looks at notes to see what to ask him next)* What exactly is a pyromaniac?

MR. PYRO gets another lighter and starts lighting it over and over again.

RAMIE: *(looks at the audience)* I'm really sorry, ladies and gentlemen, for the dilemma. *(looks back at guest)* Oh my GOSSSSSHHH! GIMME THAT!

MR. PYRO grabs back first lighter off desk and continually flicks it.

RAMIE: *(yells)* EXCUSE ME! WHAT DO YOU THINK YOU ARE DOING?! Where's my guest coordinator? I'm going to fire my guest coordinator because…

MR. PYRO: Nooooo, let me…"FIRE" him.

RAMIE: You're supposed to be telling me what a pyromaniac is and all you're doing is playing with fire.

Lights down. Light the cloth and put on the fire sound effect.

RAMIE: What's happened? Where's the lights? *(screaming)* Ow, ouch, I'm on fire. Ooh that burns. *(applies soot, messes up her hair, stumbles to the front of the desk before the lights come back up)*

Lights up.

RAMIE: *(drops and rolls, gets up and drops and rolls again while she is saying)* Drop, stop, and roll! No, roll, drop, and stop! Stop, rock, and roll! Drop, stop, and roll.

While she is rolling the lights fade back down.

END

Set: Desk and chair.

The TALK, CHAT, & RAP SHOW Series

WHO IS HE?

CAST
- Ramie, abrasive and clueless talk show host
- Mr. B, male Sunday School teacher

RAMIE: Okay, welcome to the Ralk, Tap, and the Shat Choe. Today our topic is, Who is he?" Wait a minute! Where's my guest coordinator? What kind of a topic is this? Who is he? I don't know. I have nothing to do with the guests.

MR. B enters while RAMIE is talking.

RAMIE: Who are you? What are you doing? I didn't even introduce you yet. *(talk to audience)* How can I, I don't even know who he is?

MR. B: I am your guest today. You don't have a clue, do you.

RAMIE: *(pause)* No…well I'm glad YOU know what's going on. This is MY show and I don't know who my guests are.

MR. B: I was your Sunday school teacher way back when you were in second grade.

RAMIE: *(sarcastic)* Whoopee, this ought to make for an interesting show! I mean Mr. Beasely, it's great to see you again and all…

MR. B: Thank you! It's great to be here. I want to find out if you learned anything in those Sunday school classes.

RAMIE: *(sarcastically)* If this isn't the cat's raincoat. You're going to interview ME on MY SHOW! Whose idea was this? I'm going to fire my guest coordinator.

MR. B: Settle down, it won't be that bad. I'm going to describe a character in the Bible, and you tell me "WHO HE IS."

RAMIE: That doesn't sound so bad.

MR. B: First character: He was known for taming the lions in the lion's den. Who is he?

RAMIE: He tamed the lions? Hmmm. That had to be Daniel.

MR. B: No, that's incorrect.

RAMIE: Wait, I know who it is then…WHAT! IT WAS DANIEL! WHAT ARE YOU TALKING ABOUT?

MR. B: I'm sorry, but that's incorrect. Next character: When the Israelites were fleeing Pharaoh's army, he parted the red sea.

RAMIE: That's easy, that was Moses!

MR. B: Nope. Incorrect again. I'm ashamed of you, Ramie. You were one of my best pupils.

RAMIE: *(puzzled)*…I was?

MR. B: Oh, no, I'm sorry, that was your sister.

RAMIE: Oh yeah…but you're wrong. It was Moses. You better give me the answers when you're done quizzing me.

MR. B: Okay, next character: He's a man of awesome strength, and he used his power to destroy the foundation of an arena full of evil Philistines.

RAMIE: That could only be Samson—and don't even try telling me different.

MR. B: Okay, I won't tell you that you are wrong, even though you are wrong.

RAMIE: *(innocently)* Okay…*(sigh)* Well, who is he then?

MR. B: You mean you truly don't know who he is?

RAMIE: No, I don't, and you'd best tell me the answer because YOU'RE GETTING ME VERY MAD!

MR. B: Okay, this is the last character, and it will give you the answer to all the questions. He has such great love that he sent his son to die for us.

RAMIE: This is another trick question, isn't it? Whatever I say is going to be wrong…right?

MR. B: Come on now, Ramie, he tamed the lions while Daniel was in the Lion's den and he protected Daniel. He parted the Red Sea for Moses, and he gave Samson the strength to destroy the Philistines, even though Samson was blind. It's God that works through us as long as we abide in him. John 15:5 says that without him we can do Nothing. Who is he, Ramie? Do you know him?

RAMIE: Oh sure...try and convict me on MYYYY SHOW! *(looks at watch)* Would you look at the time? Our time is up for the day. It was great having you on the show today. Mr. well...well *(look at audience)* you know who he is. This has been another edition of the Talk, Shat, and the Rap show. Thanks for joining us.

Lights down.

END

A Really Good Book

CAST
- Phil Mohair — urbane, hip, somewhat cynical talk show host
- Bill Shazzer — a clueless twenty-something with a thrashed Bible
- Harold Johnson — a pious thirty-something, carrying a white Bible in a sealed plastic container
- Jimmy Green — a fervent super-Christian with a Southern accent and a well-used Bible

PROPS
- The different Bibles
- Chairs for a talk show set

Scene: Two overstuffed chairs on a talk show set.

PHIL: *(enters with gusto)* Good evening, ladies and gentlemen, and welcome to "This is Your Faith!" I'm your host, Phil Mohair, and our topic this evening is the best-selling book of all time—the Bible. It seems like everybody wants one, but it's like dental floss—you know it's good for you, but how often do you actually use it?

To find out how America uses its Bible, we've invited three guests willing to bare it all for the camera. Give it up for our first guest, from New York City, Bill Shazzar.

BILL: *(enters and shakes PHIL's hand)* Hi, Phil.

PHIL: Good to have you on the show, Bill. Let's see that Bible of yours. It looks pretty well worn.

BILL: Yeah, well, it, uh, gets some pretty heavy use in our house.

PHIL: Sort of a coffee table book for everyone to pick up and read?

BILL: Actually, we keep it under the sofa.

PHIL: Excuse me?

BILL: Yeah, you see, one of the sofa legs broke off a few years ago, and this Bible is the perfect thickness to level it out. My family's back home watching this show on an incline. *(indicates angle with hand, then cocks head at an angle, waves into camera)* Hi, Mom!

PHIL: So you don't actually read the Bible? *(opens Bible and blows out flour sprinkled in page)*

BILL: Not exactly. I might catch a word or two when I add another photograph. *(reaches over and pulls out a photo)* Keeps 'em nice and flat.

PHIL: Great, great. I'm guessing you probably don't have a favorite passage.

BILL: Uhhh… the Northwest Passage?

PHIL: *(hand the Bible back to BILL)* Okay, then, here's one for you to look up at home: John 3:16. Got that? John, chapter 3, verse 16. You can go now, Bill.

Copyright Youth Specialties, 300 S. Pierce St., El Cajon, CA 92021.

BILL: *(while being shoved offstage)* Hey, I have an Uncle John who went into Chapter 11. Is that what you mean? *(exits)*

PHIL: Well, a guy like Bill just goes to prove the old saying that "No man is entirely worthless. He can always serve as a bad example." Let's welcome our next guest—Betty Johnson from Brainerd, Minnesota. *(PHIL becomes confused as HAROLD enters)* Not to be rude, but I thought that with a name like "Betty" you would be a woman. Bad assumption. I'm sorry. Hi, Betty.

HAROLD: No, no, I'm Harold. Betty would be the missus. She got a little nervous about appearing on your show, so she told me to come out here instead.

PHIL: Ah. No problem, Harold. Thanks for filling in. Is that your Bible in that container?

HAROLD: You bet. Betty got it from her grandmother when she was confirmed in 1945.

PHIL: An heirloom Bible. *(reaching to open the container)* Can we take a closer look at it?

HAROLD: Oh, I wouldn't do that. Betty's pretty particular about keeping this book in perfect condition.

PHIL: Well, I just want to look at it. I don't plan to write in it or anything.

HAROLD: Did you have to say that? *(yelling backstage)* Don't worry, Betty. I won't let him do anything to it.

PHIL: Let me get this straight. Betty doesn't let anyone even touch this Bible?

HAROLD: Well, we set it out when the pastor stops by, but otherwise she stores it in this here plastic container. Burps it once a week to keep the air inside from getting stale.

PHIL: Has no one ever even opened this Bible?

HAROLD: *(proudly)* No, sir. That's why it's still such a really good book.

PHIL: Ooookkaaay. Tell me, Harold, do you have a favorite Bible passage?

HAROLD: Ummm…oh, yeah: "Remember the Bible to keep it holy."

PHIL: Are you certain that's in the Bible? It doesn't sound familiar.

HAROLD: Well, I'm sure not going to open it and try to find out.

PHIL: Fine, fine. *(urging HAROLD off the stage)* Thanks for coming out and give our best to Betty. Goodbye.

HAROLD: Goodbye. *(while leaving, yells out backstage)* Hey, Betty! Your Bible appeared on TV!

PHIL: Well, folks, let's hope we saved the best for last. It seems to me the Bible would be more than a couch prop or a sequestered trophy. Our final guest comes from the heart of the Bible Belt. Please welcome Jimmy Green from Pikeville, Tennessee.

JIMMY: Brother Phil, bless you for doing this show on the Bible. When I got your call inviting me to be on your show, I was meditating on the parable of the sower and the seed. After I hung up I prayed for God's leading on whether to accept your invitation. My eye caught the very next verse in the parable: "The sower sows the word." By cross-referencing my exhaustive concordance with my word study book, I found that verse could be translated, "The sower BROADCASTS the word." As sure as hittin' an armadilla in Texas, I knew it was a sign from God that I should come on TV.

PHIL: Well, whatever. Is that your Bible in the case?

JIMMY: Yes, sir. *(removing if from the case and handing it to PHIL)* Careful now, Brother Phil. Don't cut yourself. That's my "sword of the Spirit," Ephesians 6:17.

PHIL: *(gingerly paging through the Bible)* This Bible is in pieces. *(handing it back to JIMMY)* I don't want to break this for you.

JIMMY: Have no fear, Brother Phil. "Scripture cannot be broken," John 10:35.

PHIL: You haven't been using this to hold up a sofa, have you?

JIMMY: "The young lying around on sofas will be hungry," Psalm 34:10.

PHIL: Excuse me? Sofas are in the Bible? *(takes the Bible back from JIMMY)* Psalm 34:10, you say? *(finds it in Bible)* Let's see, Psalm 34:10 says, "The young lions suffer want and hunger."

JIMMY: Whatever. "The Lord will provide," Genesis 22:14.

PHIL: You certainly seem to know your Bible. Do you have a favorite passage?

JIMMY: I get a new verse each day, Brother Phil. This Bible is better than any daily horoscope. I just open it up somewhere and point at a verse on the page. It's my leading from God for the day. I'll show you. *(takes the Bible from PHIL and opens to a random page)* Here we go. John 8:44: "You belong to your father the devil." *(confused and disturbed)* Say, I was in a bit of a hurry to pick that verse, being on TV and all. Let me try it again. *(picks another random spot in Bible)* Okay, Revelation 21:8: "Their place will be in the fiery lake of burning sulfur." Oh, nooooooooooo. *(runs off stage)*

PHIL: It seems that knowing words from the Bible doesn't guarantee that you know what the Bible is truly about. For each of our guests this evening, the Bible was a really good book. What do you do with the "Good Book" at your house? Fax your responses to the number now showing on the screen. We'll share the highlights on the air next week when we welcome three new guests to "This Is Your Faith." Good night!

END

MONOLOGS

MONOLOGS

Does your youth group's dramatic talent reside in only one or two students? Or do you want to raise interest in starting a drama ministry? In both cases, a monolog is your ticket! These one-person scripts require little or no costumes or props (though some of these monologs require a silent actor or two, with no lines)—yet they can be as powerful as a three-act play.

A CHAT WITH GOD

The monolog on page 173 might be just the mirror your students need to see that being too busy to do the things that connect them with God is the same as being to busy for God himself. *Lara Willars*

LITTLE JAKE

Abortion. The subject no one is comfortable with—nor should we expect to feel comfortable when we meet it head on with our students. The script on page 174 opens the curtains on one young woman's pain over her abortion. But given the hope we have in Christ, we can model moving through deep pain into God's gracious forgiveness and healing.

Invite one of your more refined actresses to prepare this sketch. At the end of the monologue, her face and body language should reflect the dawning peace of God even though personal pain and regret linger. *David Ruiz*

MEDITATION
JOSHUA 1:8

Coach one of your theatrical, early teen girls for this stream of consciousness monologue (page 176) that may sound all too familiar to most of your audience. *Randy Wilkinson*

MORE THAN JUICE AND COOKIES

This short introduction to Communion on page 178 makes sense to even the youngest of believers in Jesus. Invite one of your pastors to lead a youth Communion service using this model. *John Cosper, Jr.*

TO G-O-D

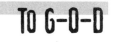

A female computer nerd delivers this monolog that dramatically highlights the pain of loneliness. You probably have all the props already—a desk and a PC setup. The script is on page 180. *Dave Tippett*

UNAFRAID

This sketch (page 182) is not for the faint of heart. Rebekah, the teenage daughter of a missionary in Somalia, tells of her father's multiple arrests for his faith in Jesus Christ. She narrates how his passion for the gospel was passed to her. The cost will be her life. Rebekah stands at a pole on the morning of her scheduled execution as she gives her monolog. The allusion is, of course, to the pole at the front of most campuses, and an invitation to "See You at the Pole" could follow the sketch. *John Cosper, Jr.*

WHERE IS GOD?

A teenage girl's prayer life get a real boost when she has to write an essay for humanities class entitles, "Where Is God?" To her surprise and delight she learns that God is closer than we think and that he's interested in communicating with us as often as possible. Her return to a childhood faith make this sketch on page 185 good for both outreach to unbelievers and encouragement to believers to connect with God anew. *Karen F. Janzen*

GAMBLING WITH GOD
ROMANS 12:1-2

A sketch on discipleship in two parts. Ham up the monologue in scene one when Kurt attempts to have his daily quite time with the Lord. He demonstrates the human tendency to justify our desires instead of truly desiring God's will. In scene two, Kurt and God (off stage) talk about what it means to be a living sacrifice. The two scenes can be separated by a talk or a reading on obedience, surrender, or God's will. (Romans 12:1-2 is a good option.) The script is on page 188. *Scott Davis*

A FRIEND LIKE ME

Sometimes it takes a strong dose of reality to make us turn from destructive behavior. Holly learned from a good friend that there's some things you're never old enough to do. In the monolog on page 191 Holly tells the story of what those things were for her. *John Cosper, Jr.*

A Chat with God

This monolog for a teenage girl needs only a telephone.

(BRENDA sits staring at phone) Please ring! Ring! *(phone rings; she lunges at the receiver)* Hello? *(pause, rushes through the conversation)* I can't talk right now, Melanie. Steven's supposed to call. Until he does, I can't think. *(pause)* Student council? Yeah, I know. During lunch tomorrow. I'll be there. *(pause)* Yeah, okay, see you then, bye. *(hangs up)*

Now will you call, Steven? *(phone rings)* Hello? *(pause; diappointed)* Oh, Jason. *(pause)* No, the Thespian Society meeting is at lunch, and I already have a student council meeting then. *(pause)* Yeah, I could do after school. *(pause; curtly)* Right. See you then. *(hangs up)*

(phone rings again; hopefully) Hello? *(pause; disappointed)* Hey, Paul. *(pause)* Wednesday night Bible study? *(pause)* No, I can't make it. *(pause; irritated)* I'm fine, I just can't make it, all right? *(pause)* Yeah, you too, bye. *(hangs up)*

(phone rings again; resigned) Hello. *(pause)* Say what? *(pause; dryly)* Right—this is God. *(pause)* Listen, I don't take crank calls. *(pause; scared)* Who is this? How did you know that? This is not funny. *(pause)* You're for real? I mean, you're really *(dramatic pause)* God! As in "Dear Heavenly Father"? *(pause; hesitatingly)* So, uh, what did you want to talk to me for? *(pause)* Oh. Yeah, I know I've been hard to get a hold of. I do have call waiting, you know. I never knew you used a telephone. *(pause)* What's that supposed mean? *(pause)* Well, yeah, I know. I've just got so many things going that there just isn't time, lately, to pray or read my Bible. *(pause)* Make the time? Hellooo! I'm in high school now. Not to mention that I'm president of the student council. When was the last time you heard of the student body president being a practicing Christian? *(pause; short, cynical laugh)* Light of the world? You haven't been down here lately, have you. Kids don't want lights these days. Christianity's a big joke to them, and I'd prefer NOT to be the butt of it. *(pause)* Yes, I know you love me. And I feel guilty about you dying for my sin and everything. But you've already done me a lot of good. I mean, I don't cheat or swear much, I pretty much do what my parents say, and I'm restructuring the student activities to include service projects and stuff. But the whole church and daily devotions thing—maybe after I graduate and my life settles down…*(pause)* What do you mean, it seems like I've run away? We're talking, aren't we? *(pause)* Wait a minute, I'm getting beeped. It might be Steven. *(clicks button)*

Hello? *(pause; joyfully)* Steven, hi! *(pause)* No, I'm not doing anything important. What's happening? *(pause)* I'd love to go to the game with you. It's tomorrow night? *(pause)* At seven. Ah, hold on a sec, would you? I'll be right back. *(clicks button)*

God? Are you still there? *(pause)* yeah, "…or forsake me." I know. But listen. I'm right in the middle of what we were just talking about. Tomorrow night is Bible study and now Steven asks me out to the game tomorrow night. What am I supposed to do? Be a nun? *(agitated pause)* I'm not saying I don't have time for you. It's just things like Bible reading and youth group and witnessing and prayer and *(stops as she hears what she sounds like; pauses with a sign; pensively)*…Just a minute, God. I…I need to end the call on the other line. I guess we do need to talk.

END

173

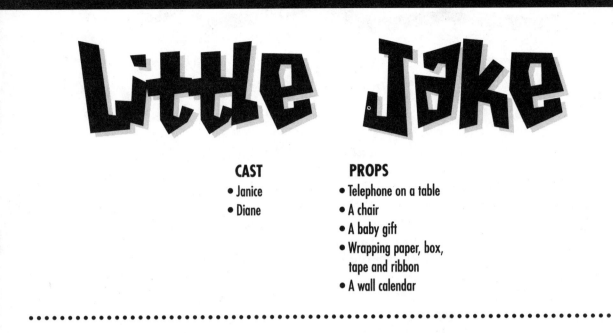

Little Jake

CAST
- Janice
- Diane

PROPS
- Telephone on a table
- A chair
- A baby gift
- Wrapping paper, box, tape and ribbon
- A wall calendar

DIANE sits at a table with a phone on it sizing wrapping paper to cut it for wrapping a baby gift. The PHONE RINGS. DIANE picks it up and speaks softly, as if drained.

Hello. Diane speaking…Oh hi, Janice…I'm all right. What's up?…Nothing. I'm just wrapping my present for Susie's baby shower tomorrow night…Yeah, I'm okay. I'm just tired, that's all. So what did you get for Susie?…Oh come on, tell me!…Oh that's perfect. I saw something like that at Nordstrom's. That is so cute. I know she's going to love it…Yeah, I think Susie is the first of our grad class to get married and have a baby…*(laughs shortly)* Well, she was made for mothering. She probably paid for her wedding with her baby-sitting money…No, that's not me either. I wouldn't have the patience. Besides, I'd have to get married first, and there's no Mr. Right for me yet…Yeah, I've got the bonfire in my calendar…um hmm, next Friday…Okay, well, you take care, all right? See you tomorrow. Bye.

DIANE hangs up the phone and tries to get into wrapping the present. She gives up, pushing the project away into a pile on the table.

God, I can't do this right now. Maybe I'll work on VBS. *(pulls calendar in front of her and flips to current month)* What's our deadline? Tomorrow the baby shower; Friday the bonfire. I've got to call to remind Amanda about bringing the s'mores. Oh, and I still haven't asked Greg to pick up the wood. *(jots down a reminder note)*…Oh yeah. VBS meeting next Saturday afternoon…And the next weekend…*(draws back from the calendar surprised)*…the singles retreat? I forgot all about it. I'll have to ask for Saturday off work. Let's see, August 28. *(begins to jot a note, gasps, closes the calendar and stands.)*…August 28…My due date. I would have been having a baby shower this week, too. *(rubs forehead and starts pacing)* God, they say you get over having an abortion. Why do I still wonder how much he would have weighed? Why does his name still echo in my heart.

(crosses arms across her body as if keeping out a chill)…Jake…I've always liked that name. It sounds strong…Something I wasn't. It seemed to make such sense at the time, but now—

God, it wasn't worth killing my baby just for the sake of keeping my reputation as a good Christian girl. Oh God, it hurts so bad when people at church tell me what a blessing I am in the youth group. I mean, that's why I had the abortion — I wanted to keep hearing those words of approval. But now those words feel as ragged and empty as my body felt after the doctor took little Jake from me.

Did he feel pain then, God? Does he still? How I fooled myself. "Fetal tissue." It didn't say "baby" to me. I wouldn't hear "baby." I only heard my excuses—it would break my mother's heart, I could no longer work with the girls in youth group, the pastor would take me off the worship team. It was always "my life." Now I wonder about his little life. I got what I thought I wanted. Every weekend I'm welcomed at church, I teach youth Sunday school, I organize summer ministries…and I hide behind a mask. I know that came with the package. Nobody's even suspected anything—not even my family.

(looking up to God)…Lord, I know I've already asked for and received your forgiveness, but it feels like I still need some other forgiveness. What is it? Let me know your grace, Father.

DIANE pauses as if waiting for an actual response from God. Suddenly her eyes get big and her hands stifle a little gasp. She registers an understanding, and seems to prepare herself for some very difficult task.

There is one person other than you and me who knows what I did, isn't there? *(presses her hands to her belly and looks up)* …Jake…This is mommy, Jake…Oh baby, I'm so sorry for what I did…Please forgive me, son…and please believe me… I love you, little Jake…I'll always love you…

DIANE walks back to the table, picks up the baby gift, and smiles through her tears. She sits down to start wrapping it, and the lights go down.

END

Meditation

Joshua 1:8

(reading from Joshua 1:8) Do not let this Book of the Law depart from your mouth; meditate on it day and night, so that you may be careful to do everything written in it. Then you will be prosperous and successful.

(looking up from the Bible) I know I can memorize this by tomorrow. No problem—I know I can. One verse—piece of cake. After all, I've got a terrific memory: *(stands erect as though delivering an important speech)* CREST HAS BEEN SHOWN TO BE AN EFFECTIVE DECAY-PREVENTIVE DENTIFRICE THAT CAN BE OF SIGNIFICANT VALUE WHEN USED IN A CONSCIENTIOUSLY APPLIED PROGRAM OF ORAL HYGIENE AND REGULAR PROFESSIONAL CARE.

Hmmm, too bad I can't just recite that tomorrow. Oh well, better get started. *(looks in Bible)* Do not let this Book of the Law…*(looks up)* Do not let this Book of the Law *(looks in Bible)* …this Book of the law—Uncle Charlie has books of the law by the dozens in his study. I wonder if he's ever really read them? *(in the voice of a judge)* An astute question, Madame Counsel.

I could be a lawyer some day. First I'd have to go to law school, probably in some far away place, probably somewhere I'd have to fly to. Flying makes me queasy. The takeoff scares me. That's when I would do all my praying. Of course, Mrs. Phillips says Christian are supposed to pray without ceasing. Oh, Mrs. Phillips. I've got to memorize this verse for her class tomorrow.

Okay. *(reads from Bible)* Do not let this Book of the Law depart from your mouth; *(looks up)* Do not let this Book of the Law depart from your mouth; Do not let this Book of the Law depart from your mouth. Now why would I want this book in my mouth, anyway? *(holds Bible over open mouth, pretending to try to fit it in)* Weird concept. But then I've seen weirder stuff in people's mouths—like those sword swallowers at the circus. How do they do that?! Talk about speaking with forked tongue. *(shivers)* Ooh, I don't even want to think about it! And those gurus that walk across red hot coals or lie down on a bed of nails— do they have some sort of supernatural powers? God has supernatural powers, but I don't think he'd waste his time helping people do pointless stunts like that. I think it says somewhere in the Bible that—oh, yeah, the Bible.

(looks down at page) Do not let this Book of the Law depart from your mouth. My mouth could sure use something cool and wet—a Pepsi would be nice. No, fresh-squeezed lemonade. The county fair has the best, but two bucks a cup is a rip off. Everything costs a lot at the carnival, especially the rides. I loved riding Orbitron. Of course if was annoying to wait in line while they hosed it out every time somebody got sick. I hate getting sick. That nasty salivating and knowing that any minute now you'll—thank God I'm healthy. It's probably from drinking lots of spring water—8 glasses a day. I wonder what'd happen if you tried drinking all 8 glasses at once? C'mon. Get on track. You've got to get this verse memorized.

Just a little self-discipline, that's what I need. But I'm so thirsty now. *(begins to stand and makes herself sit back down)* I promise I'll get a drink as soon as I memorize this verse. Mind over matter. I wonder if people really can move stuff just by concentrating on it hard enough. It was hilarious when we tried to levitate Sally at that slumber party. I never liked her—still don't. John sure likes her. What does he see in her? Anyway, he's got terrible acne. Would a chemical peel help his skin? It sounds like ancient torture. I saw it in a movie once—"Outer Limits" or some show. These guys peeled off their fake faces and underneath they were all deformed and they were worshipping this bomb as their god. No one could be that stupid. It's plain as day in the Bible that…uh-oh. *(looks at watch)* I've gotta get this memorized!

(looks in Bible) Meditate on it day and night *(looks up)* Meditate on it day and night. Now how am I supposed to meditate in my sleep? My brain's way to busy making up nonsense dreams about random trivia. What was that dream last night? I can never remember. Something about flying and still living back on 4th Avenue. Yeah, and the neighbors saw me as I flew past, flapping my arms. But they seemed stranger than me. Was that her real hair? "Hi, I'm not only the president of hair club for women—I'm also a client." Commercials. I hated the one where the guy in an eagle suit lays the egg on top of the car. "Look at those low rates!" People get paid to write stuff like that! I could be a writer someday, maybe advertising, maybe, children's books. I love that one with the llama under the bed. I saw a real llama when we took my cousins to the zoo farm last fall. You could smell it before you could see it. I wonder what it eats? I'm hungry. No. Stop it. You can't get anything to eat or drink until you finish memorizing Joshua 1:8.

(looks in Bible) so that you may be careful to do everything written in it. *(looks up)* so that you may be careful to do everything written in it. Care full. What's the opposite? Care empty? Words can sound like gibberish if you say them enough times. Like my name: Linda. LIN-DA. LIN-DUH. What kinda name is that? I wonder if Mom and Dad said my name a whole bunch of times before they stuck it on me? "Dear, let's name her LIN-DUH." It's weird to think they had a life before me. I can't imagine my folks dating, holding hands, going to a movie together. Boy, that Diet Coke at the movie theater taste like transmission fluid. What about that lemon…no. I promised myself I'd get this memorized first!

(looks in Bible) Then you will be prosperous and successful. *(looks up)* Then you will be prosperous and successful. I wonder what God thinks about those guys on TV that say you make a gazillion dollars in your spare time with no talent and no money down? Those infomercials are great—like the one where they start a grease fire on the guy's car. When you flip the switch at the car wash to wax, does it really start spraying wax, or is it just more hot water. And why is "chamois" spelled like that? I can't wait until I get my license. I hope the picture isn't geeky. Maybe I'll but my hair back so it won't frizz out. What if I can't pass the test? I hate tests. Basically I hate school—oh, no—school! I've got to finish memorizing this verse. *(takes a long, hard look at Bible, looks up, takes deep breath)* Here goes:

Do not let this Book of the Law depart from your mouth; meditate on it day and night, so that you may be careful to do everything written in it. Then you will be prosperous and successful.

Yes! I did it! Okay, God. I've done the meditation part. Don't forget your end of the bargain—I need to be prosperous and succeed in Mrs. Phillips' class tomorrow. Wow, this meditating business takes a lot out of you! *(calls offstage)* Mom, we got any lemonade? I'm dying of thirst! *(exit)*

END

More than Juice & Cookies

CAST
- Chuck, a Christian boy
- Little boy
- Two Sunday school teachers
- Jesus

PROPS
- Altar table
- Communion bread and juice
- A cup of punch and a plate of cookies
- A stack of empty, plastic communion cups

● ●

A table is set up with bread and a cup of juice for Communion. CHUCK enters.

Did you ever wonder why people take Communion? You know, the bit with the bread and the wine we do in church? It's a strange tradition for several reasons. First of all, nobody can agree on what to call it. Is it Communion, the Lord's Supper, or the Eucharist? Second, nobody can agree on how to do it. In some churches you tear a piece of bread off a loaf and dip it into the juice, being very careful not to drip it on your Sunday clothes. In other churches they pass around two platters—one with a teeny weeny wafer about half the size of a Tic Tac, the other with those little bitty plastic cups of juice. You know, the little cups that you stack up in the racks on the backs of the pews? When I was a kid we used to run around after church picking up the cups and seeing who could make the tallest stack.

LITTLE BOY enters, balancing a TALL stack of cups, which he drops at center stage. He winces as they hit the ground, looks for watching adults, sees none, then runs off.

I went to children's church and Sunday school back then. The main reason was that the teacher always served us juice and cookies.

The FIRST SUNDAY SCHOOL TEACHER enters, hands CHUCK a plate of cookies and a cup of juice. She pats him on the head and exits. He sets the plate and cup on the table.

So naturally, when I graduated to "big church," I assumed Communion was simply the grownup version of juice and cookies.

The SECOND SUNDAY SCHOOL TEACHER enters, with a communion cup of juice and a plate with one teeny, tiny wafer on it. She pats him on the head and exits. He sets the cup and platter down and picks up the wafer.

I figured they substituted the wafer for the cookies because most of the adults were on a diet.

He returns the wafer to the plate.

When I got a little older, I learned that Communion is a lot more than a mid-morning snack. Not only that, I learned that the practice of Communion is a lot older than the churches that fight over how to do it. The first people to take Communion weren't Catholic, Protestant, or Christian at all! They were Jewish — fishermen mostly, along with a political rebel, a tax collector, a traitor, and a few others. And a man named Jesus.

JESUS enters, stands behind the table. CHUCK faces the audience as if JESUS wasn't there. During the following part, JESUS breaks bread and blesses the wine as CHUCK describes Communion.

They were in Jerusalem to celebrate the Passover. After dinner that night, Jesus took bread and broke it saying, "Take and eat. This is my body."

Then he took the cup and blessed it saying, "Drink. This is my blood, poured out for you. Do this in remembrance of me."

JESUS exits.

As you can imagine, everyone was a little bit confused by all this talk about Jesus' blood and body. But they knew there had to be a deeper meaning.

They were right. Twenty-four hours later, Jesus was dead. His body was broken by thorns, whips, nails, and a sword. Trails of blood leading from the royal courts to the hill where he died and the body laid in a borrowed tomb were all that remained of the Son of God.

Jesus came to earth with nothing. He was buried in a borrowed tomb. But through his death and resurrection, he left behind a promise of forgiveness and eternal life, paid for by his broken body and spilled blood.

Communion goes by many names and can be done in different ways, but the meaning never changes. *(picks up the bread)* This is Jesus' body. *(picks up the cup)* This is Jesus' blood. He gave them for you. All you have to do is accept them.

END

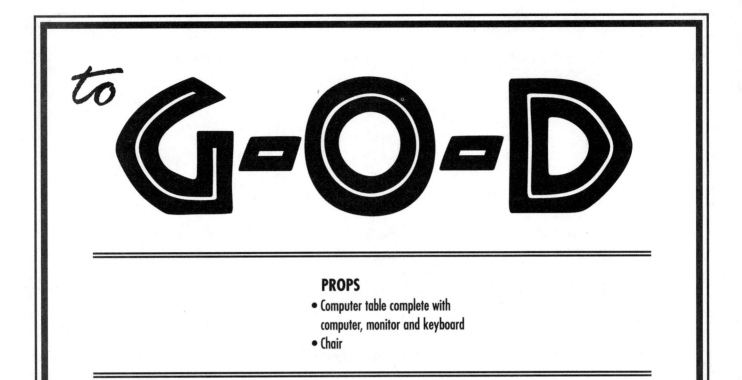

PROPS
- Computer table complete with computer, monitor and keyboard
- Chair

A female computer nerd delivers this monolog.

Set: A PC with monitor, keyboard, etc. sits on a computer table. Monitor faces upstage right. An ergonomically correct chair on rollers sits in front of the terminal. VICKI DAVIS, computer nerd, enters carrying a coffee cup. She paces a moment before sitting down at the computer and tapping the space bar to stop the screen saver. Punches a three-key sequence to open the Internet.

(after a beat) Come on, come on. The server better not be…Oh good. *(throughout the sketch, when she says she's inputting something, she hits an appropriate number of keys)* Okay, Internet communicator. Let's see…*(looks intently at screen)* Search engine… AltaVista. Keyword. Hmmm. What kind of keyword would work? When in doubt, go for the obvious. *(talks while typing)* G-O-D, enter. Processing…processing…processing. *(shakes her head and snorts)* 10 million associated references. Let's see…*(reading screen)* gods of ancient Greece…godchild…goddaughter…godparent…godson…Godzilla. I knew better than that. But what words do I use to refine the search? Why can't there just be an official web site for God? *(scrolls down the list)* Ah, this is useless. Fine. E-mail search. Enter address. Uh, how about, umm…G-O-D dot HOLY at HEAVEN dot org. Subject of e-mail. Ummmm. I'm lonely.

(continues to talk aloud as she types, sporadically) Dear GOD…Vicki Davis here… Know you're busy…thought I'd write…need some help. *(pause; now leans forward into the computer and her fingers fly)* Like, what's up with everyone these days? No one seems to

have any time any more for anyone. Even my so-called friends are too busy for me. Can't even take a minute to reply to my e-mail. In desperation I accessed the church's web site. All I got back was an electronic greeting and a request for me to fill out a visitor's card that was linked to their e-mail. Oh, and get this. They had one line for prayer requests. *(mock lament)* Oh that one line could cover all my needs. *(snorts a laugh)* I replied, "lonely," and hit send. The mail demon returned it saying it was undeliverable…the destination mailbox was full. Too busy—like everyone else.

(rises, picks up coffee cup, paces upstage) I even tried phoning a help line—voice mail. "All our counselors are busy helping other desperate people; press one if you're depressed. Press star if you have a gun at your head. I hung up. *(returns to keyboard and starts typing again)*

When I was a kid I used to write you letters, remember? It seemed more official than just praying. Once I asked you to help my mom and dad play with me more. I was lonely even then. They just got busier—until they were too busy even for each other. So I quit writing.

Now that I'm older, well, I thought maybe I would give it one more shot. Can you send someone—not through cyberspace and not through the telephone—someone with a hand to grasp my hand, with eyes I can look into, and with a friend's heart that moves them to ask me how I'm doing and then to really listen to my response. Is there any of your people who have time for old-fashioned friendship? I really think it would change my life to know someone who cared about me.

(pause; continues more slowly) That's all. Hope you get this. Not that I expect a response in any case. Therapeutic journaling is what my English teacher would call this. I'm hoping it could be more. Reply to…Vicki, at…all alone dot help.

Send.

VICKI *stares at computer as lights go out.*

END

Unafraid

CAST

• Rebekah, the teenage daughter
of a missionary in Somalia
• Passersby at the flagpole

REBEKAH, in a tight spotlight, looks haggard and dirty, with visible injuries. She is dressed as a prisoner in Somalia. She is sitting close by a pole, the top of which is not visible to the audience. During the monologue, she stands and moves still within the tight spot.

We were in church the first time I saw my father arrested. I remember the crash of the door and light from outside pouring in with the police. The other people in the room were screaming. The police shouted as they waved their guns around the room. Instinctively, my mother pulled me out a side door before they saw us. She was shaking all over, and visibly scared. She had done her best to shelter me from the government's oppression, but in a country like Somalia, you can't hide forever. As we watched my father being loaded into a van, I asked my mother why they were taking him away. Her response frightened me. "Because he believes in Jesus."

Although I was only seven, I knew Jesus loved me. I believed he died for my sins and had sent angels to protect me. Until that morning in church, I never had the slightest doubt about him. But how could Jesus allow anyone to hurt my father? Were there no angels for him? Had he done something wrong?

To my father, however, being arrested was nothing less than a blessing. My father loved the contact with other prisoners and with the guards. It gave him joy to share Christ with them. I understood nothing of his passion, at the time. All I knew was that my father belonged at home, and from my hiding place at the side of the church I whimpered for him to take me home.

My father was arrested five times! Every time, he returned home beaten and withered, usually sick. But what caught my attention was that he never came home weary. Prison fanned a fire in him that grew hotter with every trip. He brought home exciting stories of men he led to Jesus Christ—men who would never have heard the gospel unless God had allowed him to go to prison.

My father's passion for sharing Christ began to burn inside of me. One night when I was fifteen, my father came to my bedside with his Bible open to 2 Timothy. "Do not be ashamed to testify about our Lord," he read to me, "or ashamed of me his prisoner. But join with me in suffering for the gospel." *(1:8)* "You live in a world that hates God," he told me. "And it will hate you for loving him. But you must never give in. The world needs Jesus, and you must never stop proclaiming his name...even if it means death."

With that challenge, my father passed his torch on to me. The following day, my father was arrested again. We were never told whether he was shipped away or executed. Only that this time, he would not be coming back.

I knew a day would come when I would be given the choice to stand for or hide from my faith in Christ. I loved God, but I was scared of the government that stole my father; I feared what they might do to me. Then I realized, that was exactly what the government wanted. They shut my father up in prison to keep him from sharing the gospel and discourage me from doing the same. Nothing made them happier than to see me hide my faith in fear. Which is why I didn't stop to think when my chance to stand came.

Two years after my father disappeared, I led a public prayer vigil. We fully expected the police to break us up immediately, but to our surprise, the first people rushing to the scene were other believers. Christians from our town and others felt empowered to stand up for Christ. Nonbelievers hungry for hope accepted the grace of Jesus. For three days, we fasted on our knees in prayer for our families, our nation, and our government, even as they rolled toward us with tear gas and live ammunition. A dozen people died that day. Hundreds were arrested. And as one of the leaders, I was sentenced to die.

I do not regret being a missionary's daughter in Somalia. I was blessed with the opportunity to stand for Christ in a country where the gospel is desperately needed. What makes me sad is that, on the other side of the world, people have the freedom to worship God openly...and they do nothing about it. We were told all about how you in America simply don't exercise your right to worship God. Help me understand how people with unlimited access to

  183

their Creator neglect him like you do? My country built a wall between me and my God. Meanwhile you have the right to worship him in total freedom! What wall is holding you back?

Other characters walk by in a separate spot light. They carry book bags and look quizzically at the audience, as if they were doing something strange.

Is it them? Are you afraid of what they're going to think? Are you afraid to be called a nerd? They're the ones who need you to stand up the most! Maybe you're not ready for the pressure of living up to the title of Christian. Do you hide it because you're not ready to live it? Are you afraid to surrender your whole life to Jesus?

The other spot fades out. Only Rebekah is lit.

This Wednesday I will be at a pole and make my final stand. I'm not sad to leave this world. And I'm not afraid. Jesus was nailed to a pole to suffer and die for us. Maybe for some the price is just too high, but I gladly lay down my life for him.

Holy Father, keep them in your care, so that we will be united together with you in heaven. The world hates them just as the world hated you because they don't belong to it. I'm not asking you to take them out of the world, but to protect them. Fill them with your Holy Spirit. Send them into the world as you sent your disciples, unashamed, and unafraid.

Blackout.

END

Where Is God?

CAST
- Theresa (teen)
- God (offstage voice, confident but gentle)

PROPS
- Bedroom furniture
- Desk
- Phone
- Lamp

Setting: Theresa's bedroom. The bed and a lamp are stage right, and a desk is center stage. The phone is beside the bed. The door is stage left, and there's a window beside the bed.

THERESA *enters with a backpack on her shoulder and wearing a jacket. She half slams the door, kicks off her shoes, slings the backpack on the bed, and tosses her jacket on the floor. She hops onto her bed, turns on the lamp, opens up her knapsack, and pulls out her books. She looks at her assignment sheet and raises her eyebrow in confusion. She shrugs off her confusion, picks up the phone, and dials.*

THERESA: Hi, Dan?…Yeah, it's Theresa. Hey, did you get that assignment in humanities class today?…Yeah, I was wondering what's up with that! What do they mean, "Where is God?"…It's for a magazine? That's kinda weird…They probably just want to laugh at our stupid answers…Yeah, we just keep giving them what they want until they give us the piece of paper that we want. How are you going to answer the question?…yeah…uh-huh…You've really thought about this…I guess I better get going so I can come up with something, too…Yeah. See ya tomorrow, Dan…Bye.

THERESA *hangs up the phone, gets out a pen, and starts writing.*

THERESA: *(reads out loud as she's writing.)* Where…is …God? *(stops after writing the question, ponders the ceiling for a moment, then writes)* I …don't …know. *(puts down her pen, and pulls her knees up to her chest in thought)* How should I know where God is? And why does it matter? He's up there doing his thing, and I'm down here doing my thing. Who cares?

GOD: I care.

THERESA: *(raises her eyebrows and looks around; shivers)* I hate it when I feel like something's trying to get through to me but there's nothing there.

GOD: But I am here.

THERESA: *(stands up and looks around)* That's ridiculous. God can't be here. He's either way up in the clouds somewhere or part of people's imaginations.

GOD: I'm right here with you, Theresa.

THERESA: Oh yeah? *(she backs her way around the room warily and talks to the ceiling)* Then show yourself to me!

GOD: I can't. If I did, you'd die. I'm too much for you to take all at once.

THERESA: Then how am I supposed to know you're real?

GOD: Take a look outside your window.

THERESA *leans cautiously over to the window, cups her hand to the window pane and peers out.*

GOD: What do you see?

THERESA: *(leans back to bed and answers stubbornly)* The sun is setting.

GOD: And what color is the sky?

THERESA: *(matter-of-fact and unimpressed)* Red, orange, yellow, and a bit of blue.

GOD: What else do you see?

THERESA: *(peers in window again)* My brother Bobby and our dog Jack.

GOD: Do you remember when Bobby was born? He almost died because his lungs weren't completely formed yet. Do you remember what you said to me then?

THERESA: *(in disbelief)* What I said to you?

GOD: Yes, you begged me to let Bobby live so you could be a good big sister. So I helped Bobby's lungs form quickly because I thought it was best that you have the chance to be a good big sister.

THERESA: Oh yeah, I remember that now. I believed in you back then. I kinda thought you were like Santa Claus.

GOD: A lot of people have that impression of me; they haven't gotten to know me yet.

THERESA: Well, how can people get to know you if they don't know where you are.

GOD: Theresa, I'm always here. I never leave you by yourself.

THERESA: Then how come I've not known you're here?

GOD: I'm always talking to you, Theresa. I guess you forgot to listen for a while.

THERESA: I know a pastor's kid who died of leukemia. Didn't they talk to you and ask you to save their kid?

GOD: Yes, they did. But that's their story. We're talking about your story.

THERESA: So we can talk to you, but you don't really care what we say?

GOD: I care so much that I gave you the most precious thing in my heart—my very own son. I gladly embraced that family's child into heaven, but my heart wept bitterly with the pain of the family that was left behind. And I carried them through on the days they thought they couldn't make it.

THERESA: I still can't imagine why you'd let anyone go through that kind of pain if you care about as much as you say you do.

GOD: I know you don't understand, but it's okay not to understand. I've planned a unique life for you, and along the way understanding will come. Are you ready at last to turn your attention to me and begin talking to me?

THERESA: Like, you're going to be here every night for me to come and talk to?

GOD: Yes, I'm with you wherever you go.

THERESA: Cool. *(stops talking up to the ceiling, picks up her pen and paper again and begins to write)* I…don't …know…where…God…is…but…I…believe…he…might…be…closer…than… we…think.

THERESA freezes, lights go down.

END

GAMBLING WITH GOD

Romans 12:1-2

CAST
- Kurt (young adult Christian)
- God (offstage voice)

PROPS
- Lounge chair
- Small coffee table
- A coin, dice, a deck of cards and a car magazine

• •

Scene 1:
KURT enters and sits down.

Time to do my devotions. *(reaches for Bible and looks up as if praying)* Dear Lord, show me what you want me to read today. *(looks down and notices a magazine)* Hey, the new Muscle and Sports Car Trader! *(tosses Bible aside and begins flipping through the magazine, reading off car descriptions)*

Lord, I would love a new car. Lord, I need a new car. *(flips pages and reads another description)* Yeah, that's what I need, a _____ *(fill in the blank)*

Lord? You know me. I love you. You know that, Lord. I've been a Christian now for six years! You know that I only want to do what you want me to...so Lord? Show me what your will is in this situation. Okay, Lord? *(obviously thinking about how to make this work out the way he wants and then looking up when he's ready to speak to God)* I tell you what. I'll flip a coin, and if it's heads, that means you want me to buy a new car. If it's tails, you don't. *(flips coin)* Tails? *(looks up)* Best two out of three? *(flips coin again and shows obvious disappointment)*

Mmm. Lord, I tell you what. Just so I can be sure, I'll cut you for it. If I cut the deck and the card I see is a red card, then it's okay to buy the new car. If it's a black card then it means...we're not quite sure. *(cuts the deck)* Eight of clubs.

(cuts the deck again) Ten of spades. *(cuts the deck again)* Jack of clubs.

He cuts the deck again and again. Frustrated, he puts the cards down. Slowly he looks up and with renewed optimism he begins talking again to God.

Lord? You know me. I love you and I only want to do what you want me to do, and I want to be sure here that what I think you may possibly be trying to say is what you really mean. I tell you what. I'll roll the dice. If I roll a twelve, you want me to get a red car, an eleven or ten and it's a black car *(ad lib numbers and colors down to 3)* Come to papa! *(rolls the dice)* Snake eyes! *(lets out a big sigh and thinks hard)*

Wait a minute. I haven't read. Maybe I should read the Bible and find out that way what God is trying to say. *(looks up)* Lord, lead me this morning and speak to me through your Word. You know me. I only want to do what you want. Please show me your will. *(begins to randomly flip through pages)* James 1:17. "Every good and perfect gift is from above." *(smiles and flips some more)* Ezekiel 1:15. "I looked and I saw four wheels on the ground near each other." *(smiles broadly and flips some more)* Matthew 13:42. "And these will be thrown into hell where there will be wailing and gnashing of teeth." *(the smile disappears)*

Oh, Lord, if you will just show me a clear sign. Let me know for sure what

your will is. Lord send a sign. Something miraculous. Something out of the ordinary, and then I'll know you want me to get a new car. *(silence; waiting)* Nothing. Complete silence. That's odd. How unusual! That's it! What a miraculous sign. I'm getting a new car! *(looks toward the audience)* The Lord certainly works in mysterious ways, doesn't he? *(exits)*

Scene 2:

Character comes back and sits down a little more resigned. He's been listening to the reading or talk or other dialogue, and now he has a more serious and personal conversation with God who is heard from offstage or over the sound system.

Lord? I'm back. Look, ummm...about earlier. Well, I've been thinking. I really haven't been quite honest with you. I'm sorry, but I really do want to know what your will is for me. I don't mean with the car, Lord, I mean with my life. Sometimes I just get distracted, you know? What is it that you really want for me, Lord? How can I best live for you? How can I really serve you? If you would just tell me specifically what you want, I'd do it. I want to follow your plan for me, but I feel like I can never be quite sure what it is. It scares me. I want to know your will, Lord. Then I could be sure it was from you. If you would just write it on the wall for me, then I'd do it. Do you want me to keep my job or move to something else? Lord, what is your plan for me and Rachel? Do you want me to be a missionary? Lord, how can I know your will?

GOD: *(compassionately, as a father)* Give me your body.

What?

GOD: Give me your body.

What do you mean?

GOD: I want you to give me your body as a living sacrifice.

But Lord, just show me your will, and I'll do it.

GOD: You don't understand. Do you remember what my servant Paul said in Romans 2:1,2? He said, "Because of my mercy, you must offer your body to me as a living sacrifice. This is true worship. Don't be conformed any longer to the pattern of this world, but be transformed, changed by the renewing of your mind. Then and only then will you be able to understand what my will is for you."

Lord, show me your will.

GOD: Give me your body.

Show me your will.

GOD: Give me your body. When I have your body, I know I have all of you. If I have your body, I know I have the very desires of your heart, and I know I have your obedience.

Show me your will.

GOD: Why? I don't have you. Even if I did reveal to you my will, even if you were able to see it and understand it, I know that you won't obey it anyway. I can't trust you with my will yet. When you surrender your will to mine, when you give me your entire self as a living sacrifice, the you will test, approve, and understand what my will is.

Lord, show me your will

GOD: Give me your body.

I don't know if I can do that, Lord.

GOD: That's why we're talking, isn't it?

END

A Friend Like Me

CAST
• Holly, a college freshman

Lights up. HOLLY walks on stage.

Let me tell you about my friend, Emmie. I met Emmie when I was in junior in high school. Emmie was a seventh grader, and new to our church. There were a few other kids her age in our youth group, but for some reason, she latched on to me. Whenever we did something at church, Emmie always wanted to sit with me or be on my team. It was kind of irritating at first, but as I got to know her, I couldn't help but like her. She was always so cheerful, and she had the biggest smile. We became very close, and we started hanging out a lot together.

What amazed me most was the day I realized that she looked up to me, that I was her hero. Me! It seemed really weird because I had never thought of myself as anything special. But she did. She looked at me like a big sister, and she wanted to be just like me. It was, "Whatever Holly does, Emmie wants to do, too!"

We watched the same movies, listened to the same music, ate the same foods. I taught her how to make envelopes out of magazine pictures. I taught her how to be a lady and how to act on a date—and where to draw the line. The next fall when she wanted to try out for volleyball, I helped her before try-outs and then worked with her all year on her skills. She became very good very fast. Her freshman year she was a starter. Whenever I could, I was up in the stands cheering for my favorite player.

Her freshman year I was a freshman in college. I stayed at home and went to community college with four girls from my graduating class. The five of us began exploring the college scene. We split our time between the on-campus activities and Elaine's house. Her parents were so laid back. Their philosophy was they'd rather have Elaine experiment at home than in some sleazy club that overlooked minors coming with an older date.

I grew up in a nondrinking family, but Elaine's family—a well-stocked liquor cabinet is part of their lifestyle. Elaine had sipped out of her parents drinks ever since she can remember. And our friends from school loved to hang out with us there. Elaine has an awesome stereo system, a built-in swimming pool, and a great patio for dancing. So it just sort of happened that I'd try one of the guys' beers or sample a mixed drink Elaine would concoct. But I never drank too much, ever! And besides…who was going to find out what I did at Elaine's, anyway?

I don't know how it happened, but word got around to Emmie, who was still ready to do what Holly was doing. But there was no way I was going to let her join us at Elaine's. She was too young to be in that crowd. And I didn't want her trying any alcoholic drinks. She felt really hurt when I told her she couldn't come over. She kept asking, "Why?" And I had nothing to say that made any sense. What about "You can't come because those aren't healthy friends for you to hang out with"? *(sarcastically)* That would work. "You can't come because we're all walking around with wine coolers?" Try again. The bottom line was I couldn't let her come because I knew I wasn't living up to the Christian standard I told her I believed in.

I didn't realize until it was too late that Emmie could be as dedicated to following a bad example as a good one. We didn't see each other for a few days. With school and all, I didn't think anything of it. Then this morning I got a call from Emmie's mom. Emmie found someone to be her ticket to the high school party scene last night, she got drunk, and didn't get home till well after 3 a.m. Her mother was frantic. Emmie's still disoriented and can't remember much of the night. Her mother wondered if I could come over and help make sense of Emmie's recent behavior.

I'm pretty sure I can shed some light on Emmie's behavior, but that's gonna mean letting *(nodding up to heaven)* the Light shine on my recent behavior, too.

I didn't ask to be a hero, but when it didn't cost me much, I was willing to bask in the adoration. When being a hero cramped my style, I brushed off my friend.

Some hero I turned out to be, huh? *(shakes her head in disappointment, then takes a deep breath to prepare for the confrontation ahead)* I'm on my way over there now. Funny, I always thought of myself as Emmie's mentor, but it turns out that Emmie's teaching me a lesson I haven't wanted to learn. She's reflected the logical result of what I'm just dabbling in at Elaine's. I don't want to go there, and I don't want my friend to go back there.

I'm so thankful Emmie and I have another chance. Don't think I don't know that things could have ended tragically for Emmie last night. But we both have a hero who was willing to sacrifice everything to show us how to live.

END

TO THE TUNE OF CCM
(AND MORE)

Take the music many of your students listen to, and use it for dramatic purposes! These scripts each require a song by a Christian recording artist—or, in the case of a couple scripts, a mainstream song with particularly appropriate lyrics for Christians. If you own a fair selection of the last five or six years of Christian music, you probably have at least some of these CDs or music videos. If you don't have access to a modest CD collection, simply get the feel of the script and replace the song with one of your choice.

IF I'M SO GOOD, WHY ARE THINGS SO AWFUL?

One of the biggest stumbling blocks to teens is the question of evil. If God is so good and if God is all powerful, then the world the way it is now doesn't add up to God. The sketch (page 200) models an unhelpful approach for friends to take when a mutual friend is suffering. It then draws on several New Testament Scripture verses to suggest a way to find peace when the hurts in the world seem unfair.

Followers of Christ can embrace the call to share in his sufferings. As the Scriptures are read at the end of the play, show the video of the crucifixion of Jesus in either the movie *Jesus of Nazareth* or in Michael W. Smith's "Secret Ambition" video. *Scott Davis*

BETTER THAN THE REAL THING
A MONOLOGUE BASED ON EXODUS 32

You'll need the U2 music video "Even Better Than the Real Thing" to do this sketch on page 202. This visual parable makes a powerful point about our tendency to worship everything but the true God. Although the monologue can be done by one person, it's handy to have another person to start the VCR on cue. For best results, the actor must practice ahead to time the unwrapping of the TV with the start of the video. *Scott Davis*

LOWLANDS
1 KINGS 19:1-9

Prayers of distress echo among the six or eight speakers in this sketch based on Elijah's experience of isolation and depression. You'll need "Down in the Lowlands" by Charlie Peacock on his *West Coast Diaries II* CD. The drama depends on visual effect and the power of the music.

Before any speakers enter, a narrator reads 1 Kings 19:1-9 to set the mood.

One at a time, each of the six or eight speakers goes to a different spot on the stage and prays a paraphrase of Elijah's prayer from 1 Kings 19:

> *I have had enough, Lord. Take my life. I have been very zealous for the Lord God Almighty. The Israelites have rejected your covenant, broken down your altars, and put your prophets to death with the sword. I am the only one left, and now they are trying to kill me, too.*

A speaker might say something like, "I am the only one left at work who follows you, Lord," or "No one else at school obeys your commands." (There's no script.) The irony of the speakers' despair becomes clear as a growing number of speakers pray similar, desperate prayers while within an arm's length of each other.

As each speaker enters, all other speakers remain on stage, repeating their own prayers at a lower volume. After the last speaker prays, all fall silent as "Down in the Lowlands" begins with an a cappella vocal. After about fifteen seconds, when the acoustic guitar comes in, the speakers leave the stage. They cross each other's paths as they exit without acknowledging each other.

Follow up the song by commenting that, like Elijah, our sense of despair leaves us wondering if we're the only ones trying to follow God. In reality we may be merely unaware of God's work in lives around us. Conclude with a discussion on the Christian's need to experience the body of Christ, to connect with other believers who have been on our same road before. *Scott Davis*

ORDINARY AVERAGE GUY

To do this sketch you'll need the title cut from Joe Walsh's *Ordinary Average Guy* CD.

Music can communicate an intellectual concept on an emotional level. Partly because most people are more familiar with secular music, you can use popular songs to open a window on a spiritual truth. While you play "Ordinary Average Guy," a narrator reads the script when the vocalist is silent. The effect is a dialogue between the narrator and the singer regarding God's ability to work through ordinary people of faith—like Moses or the disciples. When the song is over, invite someone to read 1 Corinthians 1:26-31 from the *Good News Bible*.

The song is scripted out on page 204. The narrator reads the bold print during the instrumental bridges. To make the performance flow, the narrator's volume must match the volume of the vocals, and he must make the words fill the stated time frame. *Scott Davis*

WILL YOU NOT LISTEN?
MATTHEW 6:19-21

If your church has a deaf ministry, this sketch (page 205) is ready made to communicate the choice believers have to worship Jesus or to worship other things, people, or experiences. In view of the Cross, other gods have no place. The audience will be challenged to check their personal focus for invasion by the gods of our age.

You will need "Will You Not Listen" performed by Michael Card on *The Word: Recapturing the Imagination* (out of print). It is also available on the compilation album, *The Ancient Faith*. *Brett Hadley*

THE GENTLE HEALER
JOHN 20:30,31

Jesus is the star of this freeze-frame skit. In five scenes, timed to match the verses of Michael Card's song "The Gentle Healer," the actors portray a snapshot of Jesus healing the blind man, raising Lazarus from the dead, teaching the crowd, and dying on the cross. Scene 4 shows people looking for Jesus. The entire skit is performed using a single spotlight that fades on and off with the switching of the scenes.

There's no script—only the directions here, and you'll need biblical costumes for Jesus and 9 other male and female actors. Of course, you'll also need a CD of Michael Card singing "The Gentle Healer."

Timing is everything. As each verse of the song begins, the spotlight fades up on the appropriate tableau. Each verse gets one scene, except the last verse, which gets scenes 4 and 5. You'll need an alert operator for the spotlight. It works well to print out the lyrics with written cues for when the spotlight fade up and down.

Verse 1, scene 1: Healing of the blind person
Jesus
Blind man/woman
Blind person's friend
2 people represent the crowd
2 disciples
2 Pharisees

Verse 2, scene 2: Lazarus raised from the dead
Jesus
Lazarus
Mary
Martha
3 disciples
2 people represent the crowd

Verse 3, scene 3: Jesus Teaches the Crowd
1 person turned away
1 person leaving
1 friend inviting the leaving person to stay
Jesus
2 disciples
2 Pharisees
1 intent listener
1 curious listener

Verse 4, scene 4: People looking for Jesus
1 person asking where Jesus is
1 person saying he does not know
1 person who tries to give directions

Verse 4, scene 5: The Crucifixion
Jesus on the cross
2 people looking at the cross
1 person turned away in tears
1 Roman soldier with hammer

Brett Hadley

If I'm So Good,
Why are things so awful?

PROPS
- VCR and television monitor (preferably on a cart)
- Video segment of the crucifixion. Two options are the *Jesus of Nazareth* film, or the music video *Secret Ambition* by Michael W. Smith.
- Soundtrack to accompany the scripture
- A chair positioned in front of the TV monitor (the main character must be able to sit in the chair and not block the monitor from the audience)

ROB sits in the chair browsing the paper, obviously feeling down. SHAUN and DON enter.

SHAUN: Hey, Rob, what's up?

ROB: Oh, hi Shaun...hi Don.

DON: You okay buddy? You look terrible.

ROB: To tell you the truth, I feel terrible.

DON: What's the matter?

ROB: What's the matter? Hello...What planet have you been living on? Don't you read the papers?

DON: I've been on vacation.

ROB: There's fighting in Bosnia, starvation in Africa, murder in America, train wrecks and airplane crashes everywhere...the whole world is full of suffering, tragedy, violence, and hate.

SHAUN: Yeah, did you hear what Newt called Hillary? *(or anything else contemporary)*

ROB: I mean, look at me. My alarm didn't go off, so I'm late for work...almost lost my job. In my rush, I back into the mailbox...$300 damage. My girlfriend is mad at me, and the guys down at the shop think I'm a nut ever since I brought up Jesus during coffee break. You'd think I had a deadly infection and was contagious. I don't know what God's thinking. Maybe he's on vacation.

DON: First of all, it's not God's fault you're suffering—it's yours.

SHAUN: He's using all this trouble to get your attention. Do you have unconfessed sin in your life?

ROB: I...um.

DON: It's sin, all right. And I'll bet you haven't been in the Word enough.

SHAUN: You just gotta pray more, Rob.

DON: Now that I think of it, where were you last Sunday? I didn't see you in church...now that's your problem.

ROB: I was visiting my aunt in the hospital!

SHAUN: Yep...that's it...shoulda been in church.

DON: Well, we gotta go.

SHAUN: Yeah, Don's showing me slides of his vacation... I hear Aruba's lovely this time of year. *(both exit, leaving ROB alone on stage)*

ROB remains by himself, frustrated and thinking. At this point the soundtrack begins at background volume.

ROB: *(looking up)* Lord, I just don't understand. If you're so good, why are things so awful? I mean it seems like everywhere I look there's grief and pain...not to mention my little problems. The world just isn't fair. People get hurt and people die. Every day we struggle with temptation and the potential for global conflict or disaster. Where are you, God?! Don't you care?!

VIDEO begins. ROB is unaware of it. Spots fade on ROB. He remains seated, pondering in the dim light until the READER has finished.

READER: "Our present sufferings are not worth comparing with the glory that will be revealed in us. Meanwhile all of creation waits for its full salvation. Don't be surprised at the painful sufferings that you now experience. If you are insulted because of Christ or suffer as a Christian, praise God that you bear his name.

"I want to know Christ and the power of his resurrection and the fellowship of sharing his suffering, becoming like him in his death. Even consider it joy when you face trials, knowing that such testing perfects your faith. We do not have a savior who is unable to sympathize without weakness, suffering, and temptation. He himself suffered and was tempted, and is now able to help those who need mercy and grace in their time of testing.

"Rejoice when you participate in the sufferings of Christ, so that you may be overjoyed when his glory is revealed... when all creation will be liberated from its bondage to decay and brought into the glorious freedom of God's children." *(Romans 8:18-19; 1 Peter 4:12, 14, 16, Philippians 3:10; James 1:2-4; Hebrews 2:18, 4:15-16, 1 Peter 4:13; Romans 8:21)*

End video and fade music.

END

Better than the Real Thing

A Monologue based on Exodus 32

PROPS
- VCR and television monitor on a cart. Wrap the TV entirely in shiny gold wrapping paper (a symbol of the Golden Calf of Exodus 32).
- Music video "Even Better Than the Real Thing" by U2, cued to the beginning.

The actor reads the following monologue while slowly tearing away pieces of the wrapping paper covering the TV. Time the unwrapping to reveal the screen as the video starts.

There once was a people who grew tired of waiting for their God. "Where is he?" they asked. "Has anyone ever seen him?" And they began to wonder if the God was even there at all. "We want something we can touch," said the people. "We want something we can see."

So, bored with waiting for the unseen mystery, the people cried out to their leaders for a manifestation. "Come," they said, "let us make gods who will go before us. Give us something to guide our misguided — something that we will know is real. Give us something visible, for the God we once worshipped has become silent. Where has he gone? What has happened to him? Is he dead? Did he go on vacation? Did he ever really exist in the first place?"

The leaders of this people responded, "Offer to us your riches and jewels. Give to us your time, attention, and loyalty, and we will make you gods to follow — gods you can see, gods you can touch, gods you can relate to and understand."

Then these leaders took from the people their very souls and fashioned them into an idol of glitter and gold. "Here is your god," said the leaders. And the new god was the world.

Start video now.

The people bowed to the new god and worshipped it often. They were ecstatic. They believed this new god was real. You could see it. You could touch it. You could be mesmerized by it. "Here is where you will find truth," the people were told. "Here you will find your purpose, your values, your meaning. Here you will find that for which you were created. Pursue this. Worship this."

So the people followed, and the new god led. It took the people where they wanted to go. "Teach us," they cried. And the new god taught what the people wanted to hear. "Do what you want. Get what you want. Be what you want. Please yourself. Enjoy yourself. Elevate yourself. You can be a god, too," it said. "Do you see that you can worship yourself if you will only worship me?"

The people liked their new god. With smiles on their faces and blinders on their hearts, they brought sacrifices daily to the new god's altar. They gave their minds, bodies, children, love, allegiance, and their souls—thinking all the time that this god was real.

The Mystery, however, remains—the God of old. Although the ancient people did not see him and never again heard him, he is here. He is not silent. He is real. The god of this world is bondage; the God of the universe is freedom. You can't serve both.

Choose today whom you will serve.

END

Ordinary Average Guy

INSTRUMENTAL INTRODUCTION 0:00-0:39 Seconds	The Lord has always used men and women to speak his Word and make his presence known in the world. Even before Christ's coming, God looked for someone to speak his message. "Who can I send to the people?" he asked the prophet Isaiah. God wants his truth to be known. He wants justice to be done. He desires a righteous people. But usually, when God calls men and women to make a radical difference, the invitation falls on fearful ears. From Adam to Moses, right on through today, people frequently offer excuses instead of obedience.
FIRST VERSE 0:40-1:04	I'm just an ordinary, average guy…We're just ordinary, average guys.
SECOND VERSE 1:05-1:40	We all lead ordinary, average lives…Bowl a few frames. We're just ordinary, average guys…ordinary, average guys.
INSTRUMENTAL MUSIC 1:41-1:53	Ordinary is okay. God used shepherds and fishermen to accomplish great things. He can surely use a bowler… can't he?
THIRD VERSE 1:54-2:36	And every Saturday we work in the yard…I got a Dodge. We're just ordinary, average guys…ordinary, average guys. *(bowling ball knocking down pins)*
INSTRUMENTAL MUSIC 2:36-2:58	Now wait a minute. Enough excuses! Do you really want to rationalize away God's power and possibilities in ordinary, average lives? Moses said, "Who am I?" Jonah said, "Why me?" and Jeremiah said, "Really, I would rather not at all, Lord." But God used David—a kid; and Peter—a fisherman; even Rahab—a prostitute.
INSTRUMENTAL REFRAIN 2:58-3:59	*(fade the music)* In fact, consider God coming to earth in Jesus—a baby, born in a barn. It doesn't get much more mundane than that. The Lord isn't partial to the spectacular. Instead, he uses average men and ordinary women of faith. He uses those willing to please and ready to obey an extraordinary God! *(fade song back up for a few seconds and then out)* **END**

WILL YOU NOT LISTEN?

Matthew 6:19-21

CAST
- Walkman
- Money counter
- Two lovers
- Jesus
- A sign choir of at least two

PROPS
- Cross
- Walkman with earphones
- Five to ten $1 bills
- The song "Will You Not Listen"

Setting: Upstage center stands a full-sized cross. The sign choir stands in a V formation, midstage right. If you have only two signers, place them on opposite sides of the stage.

WALKMAN enters from stage left wearing his Walkman and reading lyrics from a cassette cover sheet. He boogies across the stage and freezes downstage right.

LOVERS, arms linked and gazing longingly and deeply into each other's eyes enter from stage right, move downstage left and freeze.

MONEY COUNTER immediately enters from stage left, intensely counting dollar bills and pausing dreamily to imagine all he will buy. He moves downstage center and freezes.

Begin playing "Will You Not Listen." A few of the SIGNERS do the first verse by themselves. At the first chorus, the rest of the CHOIR comes alive and signs in unison.

Also at first chorus, JESUS enters from stage right. He moves from actor to actor, attempting to get their attention by tapping them on the shoulder and trying to make eye contact. Each actor in turn ignores Jesus, avoiding his look and drawing back from his touch. After being turned away by everyone, JESUS looks thoughtfully at each actor and then moves upstage center. He deliberately places himself, leg by leg and arm by arm, on the cross. He pauses, recoils as if in pain, and lets his head drop forward.

Immediately WALKMAN stirs as if just awakening, looks back and forth between the cross and his Walkman. He then walks to cross, kneels, and places the Walkman at foot of cross. The LOVERS come alive, look at cross, look at each other, and then walk to cross and also kneel. Finally, MONEY COUNTER comes alive, looks at cross, and then joins the other three, placing the money at the cross and kneeling. All actors freeze.

SIGN CHOIR signs last verse of the song and freezes, making the final sign while they look at the cross.

END

SO WHAT CREATIVE SCRIPTS HAVE YOU WRITTEN LATELY?

Are your kids still talking that drama or skit you invented for last month's meeting or event? Youth Specialties pays $50 (and in some cases, more) for unpublished, field-tested ideas that have worked for you.

You've probably been in youth work long enough to realize that sanitary, theoretical, tidy ideas aren't what in-the-trenches youth workers are looking for. They want—you want—imagination and take-'em-by-surprise novelty in parties and other events. Ideas that have been tested and tempered and improved in the very real, very adolescent world you work in.

So here's what to do:

- Sit down at your computer, get your killer script out of your head and onto your hard drive, then e-mail it to ideas@youthspecialties.com. Or print it off and fax it to 619-440-4939 (Attn: Ideas).

- If you need to include diagrams, photos, art, or samples that help explain your dramatic idea, stick it all in an envelope and mail it to our street address: Ideas, 300 S. Pierce St., El Cajon, CA 92021.

- Be sure to include your name and all your addresses and numbers.

- Let us have about three months to give your game idea a thumbs up or down*, and a little longer for your 50 bucks.

*Hey, no offense intended if your idea isn't accepted. It's just that our fussy Ideas Library editor has these really meticulous standards. If the game isn't creative, original, and just plain fun in an utterly wild or delightful way, she'll reject it (reluctantly, though, because she has a tender heart). Sorry. But we figure you deserve only the best game ideas.

YOUTH SPECIALTIES TITLES

Professional Resources

Administration, Publicity, & Fundraising (Ideas Library)

Developing Student Leaders

Equipped to Serve: Volunteer Youth Worker Training Course

Help! I'm a Junior High Youth Worker!

Help! I'm a Small-Group Leader!

Help! I'm a Sunday School Teacher!

Help! I'm a Volunteer Youth Worker!

How to Expand Your Youth Ministry

How to Speak to Youth...and Keep Them Awake at the Same Time

Junior High Ministry (Updated & Expanded)

The Ministry of Nurture: A Youth Worker's Guide to Discipling Teenagers

One Kid at a Time: Reaching Youth through Mentoring

Purpose-Driven Youth Ministry

So That's Why I Keep Doing This! 52 Devotional Stories for Youth Workers

A Youth Ministry Crash Course

The Youth Worker's Handbook to Family Ministry

Youth Ministry Programming

Camps, Retreats, Missions, & Service Ideas (Ideas Library)

Compassionate Kids: Practical Ways to Involve Your Students in Mission and Service

Creative Bible Lessons from the Old Testament

Creative Bible Lessons in John: Encounters with Jesus

Creative Bible Lessons in Romans: Faith on Fire!

Creative Bible Lessons on the Life of Christ

Creative Junior High Programs from A to Z, Vol. 1 (A-M)

Creative Junior High Programs from A to Z, Vol. 2 (N-Z)

Creative Meetings, Bible Lessons, & Worship Ideas (Ideas Library)

Crowd Breakers & Mixers (Ideas Library)

Drama, Skits, & Sketches (Ideas Library)

Drama, Skits, & Sketches 2 (Ideas Library)

Dramatic Pauses

Everyday Object Lessons

Facing Your Future: Graduating Youth Group with a Faith That Lasts

Games (Ideas Library)

Games 2 (Ideas Library)

Great Fundraising Ideas for Youth Groups

More Great Fundraising Ideas for Youth Groups

Great Retreats for Youth Groups

Greatest Skits on Earth

Greatest Skits on Earth, Vol. 2

Holiday Ideas (Ideas Library)

Hot Illustrations for Youth Talks

More Hot Illustrations for Youth Talks

Still More Hot Illustrations for Youth Talks

Incredible Questionnaires for Youth Ministry

Junior High Game Nights

More Junior High Game Nights

Kickstarters: 101 Ingenious Intros to Just about Any Bible Lesson

Live the Life! Student Evangelism Training Kit

Memory Makers

Play It! Great Games for Groups

Play It Again! More Great Games for Groups

Special Events (Ideas Library)

Spontaneous Melodramas

Super Sketches for Youth Ministry

Teaching the Bible Creatively

What Would Jesus Do? Youth Leader's Kit

WWJD—The Next Level

Wild Truth Bible Lessons

Wild Truth Bible Lessons 2

Worship Services for Youth Groups

Discussion Starter Resources

Discussion & Lesson Starters (Ideas Library)

Discussion & Lesson Starters 2 (Ideas Library)

Get 'Em Talking

Keep 'Em Talking!

High School TalkSheets

More High School TalkSheets

High School TalkSheets: Psalms and Proverbs

Junior High TalkSheets

More Junior High TalkSheets

Junior High TalkSheets: Psalms and Proverbs

What If...? 450 Thought-Provoking Questions to Get Teenagers Talking, Laughing, and Thinking

Would You Rather...? 465 Provocative Questions to Get Teenagers Talking

Have You Ever...? 450 Intriguing Questions Guaranteed to Get Teenagers Talking

Clip Art

ArtSource: Stark Raving Clip Art (print)

ArtSource CD-ROM: Ultimate Clip Art

Videos

EdgeTV

The Heart of Youth Ministry: A Morning with Mike Yaconelli

Next Time I Fall in Love Video Curriculum

Understanding Your Teenager Video Curriculum

Student Books

Student Books

Grow For It Journal

Grow For It Journal through the Scriptures

What Would Jesus Do? Spiritual Challenge Journal

WWJD Spiritual Challenge Journal: The Next Level